TALLY-HO GREEN

WARREN P. WEITZEL

Llumina
Press

ISBN: 978-1-62550-376-3

I dedicate this book to my loving brother, Allen, who pushed me to write it for the family, and my mentor Joseph Zukin, Jr., who served in the 9th Division, 39th Infantry in Germany during World War II. Both are stalwart soldiers in their own rights.

Warren P. Weitzel, May 25, 2008

TABLE OF CONTENTS

Foreword	i
Preface	iii
Acknowledgments	v
Autobiography	vii
Prologue	xiii
Greetings	1
Fort Ord, Monterey	3
Junction City, Kansas	6
First Platoon, Third Squad	7
Basic Training	8
Speaking of Ropes	12
Going for a Swim	13
Infamous M&M Story	14
Basic Was Basic	15
Potassium Nitrate	17
My Mentor	18
Now the Fun Begins	20
Armor, Rivers, and Hueys	22
Packing It Up	24
Let's Get This Show on the Road	26
Anchors Aweigh	28
Welcome to Vietnam	30
Bringing in the 9th	32
Basic Load	33
Hit the Jungle Running	37
Them's Bullets	39
Combat Is Much Like Football	41
An Army Infantry Lesson	42

Combat Infantry Badge C.I.B.   43

Special Respect at Fort Sill   44

Veterans Day   46

The Bloodiest Six Months   47

Missions: Search and Destroy and   49
Cordon

Operation Niagara Falls   53

No Rain in the Army   60

Leeches, Scorpions, and Fire Ants   62

On Patrol   64

Agent Orange   66

Snakes   67

Operation Cedar Falls   70

The Queen's Army   72

Better Not Flunk Map Reading   73

The Infamous Banana Leaf Story   74

Hunker Down   75

Operation Junction City   77

Visual Imprints   96

Sgt. Weitzel's Big Test   97

Sense of Time   102

Night Ambush   103

The Fallen Seven   106

The Black Virgin   108

C-130   109

"I'm Gonna Die!"   111

The Swimming Armored Personnel   113
Carrier

Santa Fe, On My Way   115

We Never Discussed It   122

The Clock Spring   123

Fort Sill, Oklahoma   125

The Army Has a Problem   126

Let's Impress the Shavetail 128

Easy Bivouac 134

The Ride Home 135

Epilog 136

Family Military History 143

And That's the Way It Is 144

Questions and Answers 147

Mentors 158

Difficult Jungle Trail 159

Years Later 162

No, Sir 165

Soldier's Friend - A Poem 167

25-Meter Target - A Poem 168

Vietnam Letters, 1966-1980 - A Poem 169

About the Author 170

FOREWORD

Like most boys growing up in the late 1940s and early 1950s, my brother and I liked to play army or cowboys and indians. Usually the latter won out. Whether playing cowboys and indians or army, we were acting out many young boys' fantasies about being a cowboy or soldier hero. We were no different, as we played with Jim Huber and the rest of our buddies on our street. Our family had a big magnolia tree in our backyard, so when we did play army, we would pretend the magnolia pods (not yet turned to blossoms) were hand grenades. We would break off the stem of the pod and toss them like a grenade at our "enemies." A few of us saved our pennies and bought Hubley Army .45 die-cast pistols, just like army officers carried.

As we got older, we realized that we did not have far to look to find our real-life heroes. Like many fathers of our generation, our Dad had served in the armed forces during World War II, and we looked up to our Dad. He was a marine veteran of the war. Though trained as a sniper and a rifle instructor, he saw little action, as his superior officers had other plans for Corporal Paul William Weitzel. Nonetheless, Warren and I loved and respected our Dad, and we were proud of his military service. I had strong feelings of joining the military and serving my country as a marine. Many factors led to my never serving in the military. The Marine Corps was not interested in a young sniper with acute allergies. They probably thought I would sneeze and give away my position.

Looking back, and knowing what I now know of myself, it probably was best that my dream of being a combat soldier was never realized. That said, the events of my life never soured my love for history, both world and family. In the mid-1960s, when the Vietnam conflict heated up, the draft board snagged Warren for military service. As luck and God would have it, Warren returned safely to his life and family after his service commitment was fulfilled.

After he had been back from the service for a few years, I would occasionally ask Warren about his time in the military, but he was reluctant to share his stories. As we got older, we would occasionally

i

ask Dad about his military career. Sometimes, Dad would share some of the more humorous events of his time during World War II. I think that Dad's talking about some of his funnier military moments made it easier for Warren to begin talking about his Vietnam experiences, as his first few stories were light-hearted in nature. As I recall, the first story Warren told me was the "Banana Leaf" incident. The second story was the "Them's Bullets" adventure, but Warren left out the serious ending, talking only about the bullets landing by his feet.

Mom and Dad did try to tell us some Weitzel family history, often mentioning that we might have a relative who was a Civil War general. We never gathered that data when Mom and Dad were well enough to share it because we thought that we would have plenty of time to transcribe it when our daily lives were not so hectic. Our Uncle Herb (my Dad's sister's husband) was a career Military Police officer. Our uncle Warren (our Dad's brother) served under General Patton in World War II. We never knew if our grandfathers had been in any kind of military service. Mom and Dad talked often of a connection to General Godfrey Weitzel and Captain Lewis Weitzel of the Union army. We have letters written in 1862 from the family that raised our mother after her parents died when she was very young. As Dad and other family members passed before we learned and recorded their lives, Warren and I grew to understand that we had an obligation to capture what Weitzel history we could so that our descendants would not lose what links to history we did know.

I felt that Warren owed it to his son, Tim, to transcribe his story and provide it as a legacy. Warren finally embraced his obligation and, in the pages that follow, you will find his dedication to that task and above all a damn fine read. There are moments you will find the thick Asian mud sucking your boots off, as you, too, stumble through the jungle side-by-side with a brave jungle fighter and a rare human being.

Sincerely,

Allen F. Weitzel (a.k.a. Warren's baby brother.)

PREFACE

When my son, Timothy, was about ten, he asked me about my early life, and I told him that I had experienced a glorious adventure. He seemed curious, so I told him the story of how one day my "rich uncle" had sent me a letter with a great offer.

It seems that my family had, on occasion, talked about my distant uncle, but I had never met him. Now he had sent me a letter that said that he had a life-changing, fabulous opportunity for me. He had this special job for me that would take about two years, and he promised to send me to special training and schooling, which would take about seven months. Then I would be sent, all expenses paid—food, clothing, lodging, travel, medical, training, and spending money—to an exotic land in Southeast Asia. I would get to meet and interact with the local population; I would see and experience things that would change my life and that I would write home about. Very few people ever got such an opportunity, and it was an once-in-a-lifetime offer. Only a select group was given this chance.

Wow! That seemed like a golden opportunity! Here was a chance to see the world, get some free training, and have all my expenses paid. All I needed to do was promise to give my rich uncle two years of my life. Over the years, my family had sent him money each year, around April, and now my uncle was going to do something for me. What an opportunity! I had heard that this rich uncle had sent my Dad, Paul, to Hawaii for a couple of years, all expenses paid, and my blood uncle, Warren, had gotten to see Europe, all expenses paid, for two years. How could I pass up such an offer?

Then one day in April, my special letter came. It told me to pack light and go to a specific location where my journey would begin with a prepaid bus ride. I was so excited!

I must say that our Uncle Sam fulfilled his every promise.

ACKNOWLEDGMENTS

As the author, I would like to take a moment to acknowledge family and friends who helped bring this story to life, be it through inspiration, encouragement, or sweat.

My brother, Allen, has been the most interested and fascinated with my military adventures. He politely but persistently persuaded me to commit my experiences to paper. He has encouraged and supported me, guiding me through the jungle vines of writing and editing.

Joe Zukin, friend, mentor, and fellow 9th Division comrade has shared stories and experiences with me about his World War II service time in the 9th Division while stationed in Germany.

Colonel Robert Work (retired), a WWII veteran and close family friend for my entire life, was heavily involved with the history of Hitler's death. Colonel Work was in the air force and spoke fluent German. He was born in Germany, and his family fled just before Hitler took power. Colonel Work seems fascinated with my musings. Part of his story can be found in the book, *Flying For The Fatherland*, by Judy Lomax.

Ted Kopulos, Allen's brother-in-law, for his work on editing, photo scanning, and stellar book cover design. (http://www.ted.to).

Susan Weitzel, sister-in-law, lent a critical eye to key editing, the cover layout and photo section, and Susan and Allen's son, Tod, my nephew, helped with the early draft computerization.

Jim Haines, B Company, provided constant encouragement, was a diligent provider of facts and clarification, and provided several photographs to this project. He is a true combat brother.

Deborah Greenspan and her entire team at Llumina Press. All great folks to work with, including Martin McHugh, proofreader/editor, and Diane Cabral, our contact person.

Thanks to all the unheralded and unnamed fellow soldiers and contributors who supported this book effort with photos, suggestions, reviews and information, given either to Jim Haines or me, helping us make sure we provided the most accurate story we could about our time "in country."

My deep appreciation also goes out to the many people who helped with this undertaking. My son, Tim, co-workers Nathan Emmett, Sandy Turner, Sam Rangel, Jennifer Just, Nanci Burtz, and Shawn and Mike Cromwell all kept urging me on to complete the task. Friends such as Ed Hutton, Joe Zukin, and a host of others were an inspiration and offered encouragement. Cindy Field, my second cousin, Sean and Beth Weitzel, Susanne Belzer, and Dr. Robert Trifilo all sent nice notes telling me how much they enjoyed my work. I must mention Luanne Stanley, an employee at the Winchester Mystery House, where I work as the Director Of Operations, who supported this endeavor. Even Luanne's mother, Fanny Witteveen, anxiously sought new chapters before they were written.

In addition, many other people read the rough draft and offered helpful suggestions. My thanks to Major Robert Risor, James Farmer (my squad mate), Craig Moorhead, Cheryl Fallstead, Kay Frutchy, Patrick Hanna, the Cromwell family, and a host of others.

Most of all, my thanks to my fellow soldiers of Charlie Company and the First Platoon. "We came together as strangers but left as brothers."

-Warren P. Weitzel

WARREN P. WEITZEL, AUTOBIOGRAPHY

Early History

We are a rare breed; you won't find many of us around. I am referring to fifth generation Californians. My brother, Allen, and I are fourth generation-born in San Jose. Our ancestors came from hearty German and Irish stock. Living in God's country has been a delightfully warm and rewarding adventure.

Early Childhood

The country was in the midst of World War II when I was born on May 25, 1944. Much of the Santa Clara Valley was covered in orchards, whereas today it is paved over and covered with housing and is at the center of Silicon Valley. Many successful hi-tech companies, such as Hewlett Packard, Apple, Intel, Google, Adobe, and Yahoo got their starts here.

It was also the place where the great polio epidemic of the late 1940s and early 1950s started, and in November 1949, I contracted Bulbar polio. Thankfully, I was spared its devastation due to some great doctors and medical professionals.

Allen and I grew up in a house built by our father after he returned from serving as a marine during World War II. He started a business building dinette tables and chairs. The business struggled at times, so we lived a modest life, but we had a close-knit family. As a master carpenter, Dad built us lots of toys. We went to the Saturday movie matinees and watched our heroes (Gene Autry, Roy Rogers, Captain Midnight, Zorro, and others) on the silver screen. We did not get a television until 1957. We had our share of family vacations to the ocean (Santa Cruz) and mountains (Big Basin and Lake Tahoe). We had a great life playing cowboys and indians, cops and robbers, and being GI Joe like our Dad.

Friends and School

During those gentler times, neighbors bonded and children played together. In the summer, the neighborhood kids would play kick-the-can well past dark, until our parents called us home. We were in and out of each other's homes frequently. Allen tells the story about how one neighbor's mother swatted him for something he did "because she thought he deserved it." When Allen complained to our Mom, she told him that he probably had it coming. Neighborhood parents raised all the children together, and we were better for it.

Our friendships extended into school, where we all shared the same classes from grade school through high school. Lifetime friendships were formed.

Each child had daily and weekend chores to do, and we could not go out to play until chores and homework were completed.

When we were old enough to hold a hammer, saw, or wrench, our Dad would have us building, repairing, or creating things. We shared time with Dad while learning these skills.

Academics and Sports

As we entered high school in the late 1950s, the Great Space Race was in full force. Students were expected to excel academically, especially in math and science. Our teachers and parents pushed us to beat the Soviets. Our country was as tightly knit as the individual families and neighbors were.

Being physically fit was another important requirement in the 1960s. Students were expected to participate in an after-school sport or club activities. I ran cross-country track, and Allen played baseball and was in Art Club.

School Did Not Come Easy

I had to struggle in high school and college. My Bs and Cs came through hard work and long hours. One bright moment happened at the start of junior year. I was in the college prep curriculum and up against Buchser High School's best and brightest.

Mr. Bailey was a tough English teacher. The second week of class, he handed back essays we had written, and he was on the rampage. "You students are college bound, and this is the best you can do? You have disappointed your parents, the school, and me. Out of thirty-four students, seventeen of you received an F, fifteen received a D, and only two of you got a satisfactory grade of a C minus."

He then passed out the papers, addressing each of us by last name (he had been a captain in World War II). You could hear moans and groans from the student body and class officers, varsity team members, and other high achievers. Nobody was happy with his or her failing grade. Mr. Bailey was slamming us hard! People were whispering to each other, asking what grade they had received.

When he got to me, Mr. Bailey put the paper face down on my desk. I turned it over to look at what I was sure was going to be an F, but I saw a red C-minus. I was in shock. People around me asked what grade I had gotten, and embarrassed, I mumbled, "Not too good." I did not share my achievement. I was afraid it would suddenly vanish, and I did not want to jinx it. I do not think I even told my parents; I was in academic shock!

I still struggle with grammar, punctuation, proper tense, syntax, hackneyed expressions, and a host of other writing *faux pas*, which is ironic, since 75 percent of my job requires writing. My scholastic efforts paid off, however; I graduated in the top third of my class. In college, although I had to work hard, I made the accountants' honor society before Uncle Sam told me he needed my skill sets in Southeast Asia.

Management and Leadership

When I got my first car, a '50 Ford, I became one of the cool-car guys in the student parking lot, and cheerleaders, song girls, and others wanted to ride in my pure white Ford. It had a cool set of wheels, red Naugahyde upholstered seats (that Dad had made for me), ivory dashboard knobs, glass-pack mufflers, '57 Olds spinner hubcaps, Lakes pipes, a front-end rake, and a smooth running V-8 engine. Mr. Heilman, the school's assistant principal, could not quite adjust to the quiet and studious Weitzel driving around in such a souped-up machine.

I needed gas money, however. After cutting lawns for a year, I got a summer job at a newly opened amusement park, Frontier Village. Disneyland had opened in 1955, and Frontier Village followed in 1961. I quickly advanced at Frontier Village from groundskeeper to ride operator and then to supervisor, manager, and director of operations.

I applied classroom discipline to my work. I was fortunate to have had great teachers in and out of the classroom. Working with my parents at their dinette business and learning from great mentors at Frontier Village, such as Joe Zukin, Ed Hutton, and Keith Kittle helped me develop my management and leadership style. I have taught my ethics, skills, and graces to the thousands of employees under my charge, over the years. I have codified my lessons in hundreds of employee manuals and leadership training classes. My philosophy is that we get the employees and the children we deserve.

Higher Education

After Vietnam, I did not return to San Jose State. I was one unit short of being a senior, but I decided that I wanted to stay in amusement-park management and not become a pencil-pushing (no computers at that time) accountant.

I loved working with people, helping them to grow, develop, and blossom. Life and the world of business were teaching me so many great lessons; I had found my niche.

I was learning many technical skills and life's three most important disciplines: communications (reading, writing, speaking, listening, body language, and the light touch—assurance), human relations (it is all about people), and problem solving (life is a series of choices).

It has been said that successful people either know what they are doing or they fool an awful lot of very intelligent people. I do not know which axiom applies to me, but for forty-nine years, I have made my mark as the director of operations at Frontier Village Amusement Park and currently at the world-famous Winchester Mystery House. I have learned so much from my many friends, employees, and business associates. They are the source of a wealth of life and business lessons.

Great Losses

Everyone experiences great losses in life, and I have had my share. I never got to really know my grandparents as much as I would have liked. Losing one's parents is always a tragedy; a library is lost.

My loving wife, Debbie, died early in our marriage. The ravages of several deadly diseases were too much for her to bear. Our son, Timothy, was only six when Debbie died. We missed her; life was a struggle for both of us due to my long and unusual work schedule, but we made it. Tim is living in Texas with his lovely wife and princess daughter, Samantha.

Blessed

I look back on the many events in my life and marvel at the blessings that have been bestowed upon me. I'm lucky to have been born and raised in a most desired spot in the world, the Santa Clara Valley; to have had loving parents; a fantastic brother; caring relatives, friends, and neighbors; good health; and a loving son and wife. Blessed, truly blessed.

My upbringing and life experiences have given me a good mind, motivation, and a sense of values and ethics. My many mentors have kept me focused and headed toward the Emerald City on life's Yellow Brick Road: the five equities of financial, spiritual, sociological, physical, and philosophical.

I enjoy my leisure hours by reading the classics from my vast library. "Read books for all time, not just the moment."

Life's Many Lessons

I follow some great advice in not trying to reinvent the wheel. I have taken the lessons from many others and woven them into the tapestry of my own life. It has proven to be a successful approach and has led to my own collection of Warrenisms. Here are just a few life and business lessons others have taught me:

Allen (brother) "Every situation in life has its funny side. Find it and laugh at it.

Beatrice (mother): "Always say thank you in person or in a note."

Paul (dad): If you don't help other people, then what's the purpose of your life?"

Debbie (wife): "Don't share your problems; make other people feel good about themselves."

Timothy (son): "Dad's Zen mask is scary. I didn't know whether to talk to the alien or run away."

Mr. Bailey (junior-year English teacher): "Always do your best work; if not now, when?"

Keith Kittle (Winchester Mystery House general manager): "See the big picture, but pay attention to the details."

Ed Hutton (great friend): "You won't get rich working nine to five. You've got to have multiple streams of outside income."

Joe Zukin (my Socrates): "Don't compromise your ethics, values, or standards. Continue to become better each and every day."

Captain Risor (military leader): "Take care of your men. You need them—"

Lieutenant Walker (military leader): "—more than they need you."

So many lessons learned; so many more to master. Should we live our lives through our experiences or through our capacity to think? The story you are about to read transports me from my secure and comfortable roots in the orchard heartland of prunes, apricots, and walnuts known as the Valley of the Heart's Delight, to Hell's Backyard in the steamy and hostile jungles of Vietnam and back home again.

PROLOGUE

For years, the family, mainly my brother, Allen, has been after me to record my military history and my time in Vietnam. I had generally resisted, but recent persuasive tactics and family events have caused me to relent.

I must caution you that some of the material is raw and gritty and may not be suitable for all readers. If you choose not to engage yourself in the fascinating adventures of one of God's Lunatics, no hard feelings.

For the readers' convenience and to eliminate any confusion about the time of day of these events, I have tried to avoid the use of the military clock (except when quoting another soldier).

This book is the story of one man's two-year conscription into the army at the height of the Vietnam War; his training experiences and jungle warfare encounters with the enemy, elements, and hostile environments. The graphic combat stories have been supplemented with the details of daily hardships encountered by this lowly combat infantryman.

I hope you enjoy these humorous, scary, and in-your-face stories that up until now have remained hidden from the interested audience. If you have ever wondered what it was like during those times, you'll have an opportunity to peek behind the jungle curtain and learn the stories of this "shake 'n bake" infantry platoon sergeant. Tally-Ho Green!

Warren P. Weitzel

GREETINGS

I knew the "letter" would be coming soon, that is to say, the greetings from my Uncle Sam. It was the spring of 1966, and the Vietnam War was in a big buildup phase. General Westmoreland was asking President Lyndon Johnson for more troops in order to stop the Communist aggression in Vietnam.

I had been attending San Jose State, majoring in accounting. Student deferments were granted for those taking fifteen or more units, but I was carrying only twelve units because I was working forty hours a week at Frontier Village Amusement Park.

The letter arrived the first week of April, and I had orders to report to the induction center in Oakland on April 26. The letter said that a bus would take us from the army recruiting office on the Alameda in Santa Clara to Oakland. I remember that Dad drove me down at 5:00 A.M. on a dark and quiet morning. I was thinking that my world was about to change in ways I could not imagine. We said our goodbyes, and Dad told me to take care of myself and that he was extremely proud of me.

Forty guys and I waited in quiet solitude to board the Greyhound bus. About 8:00 A.M. we arrived at the induction facility, which was filled with hundreds of young men looking a little dazed and scared. After filling out some paperwork, we stripped down for our physical exams. We moved from station to station in our underpants as the doctors and medics checked our heart, lungs, eyes, mouth, height, weight, and butts. I was just shy of my twenty-second birthday and slightly older than most of the guys.

We got dressed and took a battery of aptitude tests, and then we waited in line as our tests were graded. I remember the sergeant looking up at me and saying, "You got a ninety-one; you're one smart kid!" He closed the test folder, handed it back to me, and directed me to a waiting bus.

Not everyone went to the bus. Some guys were directed through another door. (To nowhere?) But, forty of us boarded a bus for the two-hour ride to Fort Ord in Monterey.

1

FORT ORD, MONTEREY

As the bus came to a stop in front of some weathered, faded yellow buildings, a tough- looking sergeant with lots of stripes on his arm boarded the bus and said, "Welcome to Fort Ord. You've got fifteen seconds to get your asses off this bus and lined up on the yellow lines. Now move it!" I did not know it was possible to empty a forty-passenger bus in fifteen seconds.

We sure snapped to attention! We were told to look straight ahead and not to make a sound. Then for the next several minutes—as one sergeant shouted out a laundry list of instructions and requirements—the others slowly walked up and down the line of recruits, carefully looking over each one of us and sometimes making general, demoralizing comments about our looks, physical stature, hair length, or other individual characteristics. They had begun the effective process of tearing us down to the lowest level before rebuilding us into combat-hardened fighting machines.

After that first cultural shock, we took another battery of written tests, and then we were marched to the mess hall for our first taste of army chow. It was not too bad. We had fifteen minutes to eat before "falling in" for our march back to the barracks. Everything was done in formation style. March to this place and march to that place.

The first night in the barracks and doing fire watch were quite a surprise. Someone had to stand fire watch in the barracks for an hour and then wake up the next guy for his turn. All of this was part of the process of breaking us down.

Imagine going to the latrine and stepping up on a raised platform with eight toilets all lined up, spaced about two feet apart. No dividers, just guys sitting, doing their military business, while others waited their turns.

It was cold and foggy in Monterey. We would be awakened at 4:30 A.M., have thirty minutes to shower, shave, make our bunks, get dressed, and fall out for reveille. Then we had thirty minutes of exercises—running, a daily dozen jumping jacks, crunches, push-ups, and the like.

3

Finally, at 5:30 A.M. came breakfast. We would march to the mess hall, stand in line at attention, file in, move our tin trays along the chow line, eat quietly at long tables, and then fall out into formation for the march back to the barracks. We were allowed ten minutes to clean up, get our gear, and fall in again for the day's ten hours of activities.

The first week was busy. We got our uniforms and shots and learned how to salute, make a bunk, fold clothes, march, address officers, shine shoes, organize a footlocker, wear a uniform, clean a barracks, memorize the general orders, and generally become a presentable soldier.

It was interesting how uniforms were issued. You would ask for a certain size, but they would give you something either too large or too small. Within the first week or two, however, you would discover that the article was fitting nicely. Uniforms were issued based on your height. Weight did not make any difference, because as the diet and exercise programs began to take hold, everyone soon had the same physique. The teardown process and exercise program were effective.

The sergeants were always shouting commands, often right in our faces. We were never physically touched, but they were always eyeball-to-eyeball or nose-to-nose with us if anyone needed "personal" attention concerning a given command, instruction, or order.

The idea was to tear at our self-esteem and psyche in order to get us to forget who and what we were. They wanted us to become something different from a thinking civilian. They were beginning the process of making us into highly disciplined, action-oriented, quick-responding combat infantrymen—trained, hardened killers.

While we would stand at rigid attention in formation, the sergeant would slowly move up and down the ranks, stopping inches from each recruit's nose, shouting out an order to recite a specific general order or command. If a recruit hesitated or faltered, he would be ordered to drop to the ground and give the sergeant twenty-five push-ups in a loud count. The goal was to have everyone doing push-ups, and we are not talking your wimpy high-school variety. These were the "upper arms parallel to the ground and chest touching the ground" type.

There was no talking, no noises, nothing but the loud counts of GIs reciting orders or counting out push-ups. The same ritual would take place in the chow line. As recruits would stand in line, the sergeants would move up and down, inspecting uniforms, asking for recitations, or ordering push-ups.

Oh, and exercises. We would run thirty minutes before breakfast, calling out the cadence responses to the sergeant's chants. These were followed with more calisthenics of the hard-core variety. They made you sweat. However, these were merely the warm-up to what was to come.

We were not permitted to keep any personal items such as clothes, pictures, teddy bears, or jewelry. Everything—and I mean everything— had to be packaged up and mailed home. We were supervised closely under the sergeant's watchful eye.

Packages in hand, we were marched to the base post office, where Uncle Sam graciously paid to have all of our earthly possessions shipped home. All ties to the outside world were being cut.

We were required to write a letter home, and for those who needed help composing one, a "friendly" sergeant was close by to tell us what to write. A "caring and considerate" sergeant carefully supervised everything we did—even showers and hygiene. The smallest detail of our lives was under scrutiny of the concerned military. Our lives were structured and rigid; the commands were loud and crisp; we were well fed and given eight hours of sleep each night, but some of those caring concerns were about to change—especially the eight hours of sleep and our upcoming Advanced Individual Training (AIT).

After a week of teardown, we were instructed to gather our gear, what little we had, and then we were marched three miles to the base train depot to board a train for the two-and-a-half-day ride to our new home in Junction City, Kansas, home of the newly reactivated 9th Infantry Division.

It was a most enlightening experience. The scenery was beautiful, but being confined for sixty hours with sixty guys was a cultural shock and life lesson. Guys can be crude, raw, and blunt, but the bonding can also be strong. We would have to line up for the lone toilet (no shower) in each car, and we would go in formation to the dining car. The rest of the time was ours to read (what?), play cards (who had cards?), sleep, and enjoy our last few hours of free time. What awaited us in Kansas would be anything but relaxing. Oh, one thing for sure: we would see lots of scenery on the plains of Kansas.

JUNCTION CITY, KANSAS

Our train arrived at 1:00 A.M. in Junction City, Kansas. We disembarked and climbed aboard the caravan of deuce-and-a-half (two-and-a-half-ton) trucks waiting to transport us to our new home. They rolled across the Kansas prairie, filling the night air with their diesel exhaust.

As our caravan pulled onto the battalion grounds, a band (actually it was piped-in music) was playing some military marches. We disembarked and formed up into platoons as our names were called off. I ended up in First Platoon, Third Squad of Charlie Company.

Lieutenant (later Captain) Risor was standing with his officers and the top sergeant, Tops, as he was affectionately known. The lieutenant greeted us with a nice speech. He told us of the proud World War II history of the 39th Infantry, 9th Infantry Division.

Our motto was "Anything, Anytime, Anywhere, Bar None." Our divisional shoulder patch was a red-over-blue Octofoil. Our division had recently been reactivated, and we were going to be training as a full division. This was something that had not been done since World War II, some twenty-one years earlier.

Ours was the second of four regimental units to start training. Our own artillery, helicopters, and transportation units supported us. Lieutenant Risor did not know our ultimate deployment, but he did know that we would be training hard and that much was expected of us. We had some seasoned leaders (officers and noncommissioned officers) overseeing our thirteen weeks of basic and ten weeks of AIT (Advanced Individual Training). After that, we would train as a whole division, focusing on jungle warfare.

Fort Riley was the home of General George Armstrong Custer and General George S. Patton, Jr., and we wondered which infamous general our training would emulate.

FIRST PLATOON, THIRD SQUAD, CHARLIE COMPANY, 39TH INFANTRY

For those readers not in the know, here is brief break down of how the Army sectionalizes the men.

SQUAD: 10–12 men. We had three rifle squads and one weapons squad (machine gun and mortars) in each platoon.

PLATOON: 40–44 men. Four squads made up a platoon. Each squad had a squad leader, a grade E-5 buck sergeant. A platoon, 40 soldiers, has a platoon sergeant, grade E-6. (The "E" stands for enlisted. A commissioned soldier is an officer—lieutenant.) If an E-6 is not available to be a platoon leader, the senior E-5 (buck sergeant) will step in as platoon sergeant.

COMPANY: 160–168 men. Four platoons to a company. First Lieutenant Risor was Charlie Company's commander.

BATTALION: 900 men. Five companies to a battalion.

REGIMENT: 4,000 men. Ours was the 39th Infantry. Four or five battalions make up a regiment.

INFANTRY: Besides the infantry regiments, of which we had three (39th, 47th, and 60th), there are other logistical and combat units, such as armor (tanks), airmobile, transportation, medical, supply, quartermaster, and assorted smaller units.

DIVISION: 15,000 men. Ours was the 9th Infantry Division.

CORP: Three or four divisions to a corp. We were in III (3rd) Corp in Vietnam.

BASIC TRAINING AT
FORT RILEY, KANSAS

Basic training was a hectic, thirteen-week course. We were on the go sixteen hours a day, but it was not terrible. Some guys got homesick and were not savvy enough to learn the ropes, but once everyone else figured out the game and rules, it became an interesting exercise. Perhaps being twenty-two gave me a little edge. I was appointed acting squad leader (ten guys).

The biggest shock was the crudeness of some of the "hicks" from the South and from the hills of Arkansas. They did not bathe or attend to personal hygiene, and it was a struggle to get them to shower, clean their bunk space, and behave like soldiers. Somehow, we were able to teach them proper personal behavior, and they turned out to be able combat soldiers.

The training was challenging but not unbearable. We ran, did calisthenics, climbed ropes—lots of rope climbing—ran through water and mud (lots of mud), sat in field classroom bleachers, and practiced military discipline. And, oh, the inspections!

I was good at the theory stuff, such as map and compass, inspections, military justice, and leadership, but I did not fare well with pugil sticks. That exercise required our getting suited up in football helmets and heavy gloves and carrying big sticks heavily padded at each end. We would pair off and go at it until one of us was on the ground, knocked senseless—it was usually me.

After a few rounds of battling different opponents came the log-over-the-water exercise. Two guys go at it on this big log over a muddy pit. If you ended up in the pit, you would have to go at it again until you knocked someone else into the muck. Like I said, this was not my strongest discipline, and I spent many times climbing out of that pit.

Cleaning? We were always cleaning. Get dirty, clean up—ourselves, clothes, rifles, web gear, boots, equipment, barracks, the compound, and everything in between.

The days were long, but we were given eight hours of sleep, and falling asleep was not difficult. After ten or twelve hours in the field, we had two or three hours of cleaning before lights out.

We would dig foxholes and then move them. That was always lots of fun—Not! Learning how to fire and care for our weapons and toss grenades (fragmentation, concussion, and smoke) is not as easy as it appears in the movies. Pulling out grenade pins is not easy; they are stuck in very tightly so they cannot be accidentally caught on a branch in the jungle and unintentionally yanked out.

I remember one incident in Vietnam. We had set up for a night perimeter, and we heard movement in front of our position. (We happened to be in a heavy Viet Cong stronghold area.) We decided to toss a grenade, but five of us could not get the darn pin out. We passed that thing around two or three times, but the pin would not budge. Someone finally did get it freed up, but if it had been the VC, we would have all been dead by the time we finally tossed the friggin' grenade.

We trained and qualified with the heavy, wooden-stock M-14 rifle. It weighed eleven and a half pounds. Eleven pounds does not sound like much, but try carrying one around for sixteen hours a day. It gets darn heavy!

About six weeks into basic, we got M-16s, a hot-firing, rapid-discharge weapon that was just starting to be used in Vietnam. It had several problems, however. It was designed as a dry-fire (no lubrication) weapon, but that did not prove to be the reality. The thing would jam, so we started using a light lubricating oil. Guess what? As we would soon discover in the heat, muck, and dirt of the Vietnam jungle, light oil did not work either. We ended up begging for 90-weight tank oil from the guys on the M-60 tanks and armored personnel carriers. The stuff was like glue, but it would not wash off in the rain and the otherwise wet conditions we constantly faced. The 90-weight oil seemed to be the permanent answer.

The M-16 was a wicked killing tool. Lightweight, it would fire off a twenty-round clip in five seconds. When the bullet hit a person, it would enter like a normal round but would then begin to tumble, causing lots of tearing damage. We learned how to clean, repair, assemble, disassemble, and love that baby. It was our single most important lifesaver in the hostile jungle.

The M-16 was actually my preferred weapon. Although we were highly trained in a variety of killing implements—hands, knives, bayonets, light weapons, explosives, and calling in artillery—I preferred the M-16.

The M-14, a much heavier weapon, was bulky and had a longer barrel and stock. The M-16 could be fired from the shoulder, hip, or even over the shoulder with just one hand. Not so with the M-14.

Hand grenades were good explosives but not much use in the thick jungle vegetation of Vietnam. We had both the flesh-tearing fragmentation (WWII-type pineapple), and the newer, smooth-skinned concussion type with sharp wire, shards, and explosives neatly packaged on the inside. I can recall only a handful of times that we used grenades in the jungle. We did use them for booby traps for our Claymore mines but seldom tossed them at the enemy. The enemy was always too close for a grenade.

We used our bayonets for a variety of purposes—like cutting vegetation, digging out leeches, opening cans of food and boxes of ammunition, and occasionally we fixed them to the end of our M-16 for close infighting with the Viet Cong.

Claymore mines were a great defensive weapon. We would set them up at night around our perimeter or field-of-fire positions. We could activate them with a blasting cap electrical charge—and they were a wicked device filled with shrapnel that maimed if it did not kill.

Unfortunately, we had a few serious accidents when guys accidentally fired off a Claymore. One of our first kills was a "friendly fire" discharge of a Claymore when a guy taking a dump out in front of a foxhole position was mistaken for the VC, a sad situation.

Claymore mines are made with plastic explosive, C-4, a clay-like substance packaged in two-pound bricks for easy carrying. An electrical charge will set it off, but it will also burn like natural gas when lit with a match, making a warm, pretty blue flame. We used it to blow up trees, tunnels, stashes of ammunition, and a host of other destructive activities. It is the GI's friend. Nobody complained about carrying extra C-4.

Oops, I'm getting ahead of myself. I preferred the light M-16, but other weapons were needed in jungle warfare.

Our day began at 4:30 A.M. and did not end until 8:30 or 9:00 at night, except for those night field exercises. We did many day and night hikes in addition to the famous twenty-two-mile hike fully loaded with combat gear.

We practiced night maneuvers and live-fire attack drills, and we did lots of guard duty—sometimes in 22-degree weather—and dug foxholes.

(The fun part was when a sergeant did not like where you had dug your foxhole and wanted you to move it three feet in another direction.)

Among the dozens of other skills we learned, practiced, and mastered were crossing streams hand-over-hand on a rope, setting up field-of-fire positions, throwing hand grenades, assembling our rifles in the dark, hand-to-hand combat, bayonet killing, pugil stick fighting, gas mask drills, target practice, and forging rivers and streams. We also climbed ropes, rope ladders, and fifteen-foot walls, and we learned to read maps, jump out of helicopters, use a compass, and work as a cohesive team.

These and other disciplines and skills were drilled into us, and maybe if we did well any one-week and passed our Saturday inspection, we would get a half-day off on Sunday, but we were still restricted to the company compound. We could go to church (strongly encouraged), read, maybe go to the recreation hall, or just lie in our bunks.

About the third week of basic training, I was called to the captain's office, and he sat me down for a talk about going to OCS—officer candidate school—to become a 2nd lieutenant. Although it was an interesting and flattering offer, I was not looking to add another year to my military service. I just wanted to do my duty and get back to being a "cowboy" at Frontier Village in San Jose.

SPEAKING OF ROPES

Running, push-ups, and rope climbing were common exercises in basic training. We ran daily, and push-ups were done while waiting in line for chow. The platoon sergeant would walk along the line and every Xth guy had to drop and give the good sergeant twenty-five push-ups with loud, distinct counts. All that paid off when it came to the weekly rope climbing.

Twelve-, twenty-, and thirty-two-foot-high poles dotted one field, and bars stretched between them with heavy-duty hemp ropes hanging above sandpits. We started climbing the twelve footers and graduated to the thirty-two footers by the middle of basic training. The last three weeks we were all climbing the thirty-two footers with our full combat gear, sans M-60 machine gun rounds.

Trainees quickly learn the trick of rope climbing and descending. After the first hand-rope burns, one quickly learns how to descend without scraping off all the hand skin.

GOING FOR A SWIM

We had swimming tests, and those who could not swim received special training after Saturday inspections. I was a fair swimmer, but none of us were ready for the sergeant's humor one day. We had just come back from a heavy morning field exercise, and after lunch we fell into formation; the sergeant barked out that since we had done so well that morning, we would get a treat and go for an afternoon swim. This was an odd thing, because the army does not normally tell you what you are going to be doing; you just wait and see what's in store.

Some of us thought it was odd that we had on full combat gear, but off we marched to the base, super-sized swimming pool. This thing was huge—an oversize Olympic pool. Okay, we think to ourselves, we will strip down to our skivvies and have a nice relaxing swim. Oh no! We were lined up, in full combat gear and M-16s, and told we would have to swim the length of this pool. Every ten seconds, the sergeant yelled "Jump!" and ten guys jumped into the deep end, splashing water and trying to stay afloat for fifty meters. A couple of guys had to be rescued by the lifeguards, but after a couple of tries we all made it.

The interesting thing about basic training was that you had to pass every discipline (swimming, rope climbing, helicopter rappelling, marksmanship, map reading, hand-to-hand fighting, physical fitness, twenty-two-mile march, and a hundred other things) or you did not pass basic training. There was no room for anyone who was not physically, mentally, and emotionally fit for the task. A few guys washed out, but overall we were a tough unit. After all, where we were going, the test was for real—no second chances.

THE INFAMOUS M&Ms STORY

The First Platoon's leader was Lieutenant Leslie, a large man of color who was tough but fair. He worked us hard to become the best platoon in the company. He wanted First Platoon to be the *first* platoon. I suspected that he wanted to be a career officer and was looking to make his mark as a true leader.

After four weeks of basic training, we were given our first outing to the PX (post exchange) in order to buy our basic needs—shaving gear and cigarettes. I did not smoke, but I had other things in mind. We were told in no uncertain terms what we could and could not buy. Candy and cookies were out. We had just fifteen minutes to get in, buy, and fall back into formation.

The PX was huge—like today's Costco. Aisles and aisles displayed everything one would need. Fifteen cash registers were ringing up sales. I got my basic supplies, and then I found it! I came across the cookie and candy aisle. For a sugar-starved GI it was heaven! Oh, the temptation was too great, so I loaded up on Oreos and a couple of pound bags of M&Ms. I looked around for Lieutenant Leslie and saw him standing at the far end of the checkout lanes, so I went to the other end to pay for my cache.

We marched back to the barracks, and we were given five minutes to stow our stuff and fall back into formation. Being a "smart and crafty" squad leader, I decided to hide my contraband sweets in my laundry bag, which was tied to the end of my bunk—a safe bet. Yeah, right!

We marched to the mess hall for lunch. Upon returning to our barracks, we discovered the place a complete shambles. Bunks, lockers, and sea chests were overturned, and the place was strewn with clothes, toiletries, and magazines. My M&Ms and Oreos were covering the entire floor, all smashed to smithereens.

And there, standing at the far end of the barracks, arms crossed, was the big, black, Lieutenant Leslie looking none too happy. Without a word, we knew our afternoon assignment. That is one lesson we quickly learned. Lieutenant Leslie's word was law! I never had any trouble with the good lieutenant, but I think that day he lost a little respect for me. I had disappointed him, and we both knew it.

BASIC WAS BASIC

Basic training is designed to develop the GI (government issue) soldier into a physically, mentally, and emotionally fit fighting machine. We were trained to react, not think. One did what one was told, immediately and without hesitation—thinking would come later.

On one occasion, we boarded a Chinook 47 (twin rotor) helicopter. Boy, are those things loud inside. We sat in our web seating, fully loaded with our combat gear. When we got to our destination, the crew chief lowered the back loading ramp, and two guys threw out this seventy-five-foot rope ladder.

Sure, earlier in the day we had seen a movie about the procedure, and we had practiced climbing down such a ladder slung over the side of a wooden wall with a sand pit at the bottom, but we had no idea we would be doing it from seventy-five feet in the air, with massive forces of prop wash pushing down on us as we dangled from a swaying hunk of rope. That was it about the army! You were seldom told in advance what you would be doing next—lots of "keep you guessing"–type training.

We were ordered to stand up, approach the end of the open ramp, kneel down, and one by one start climbing down the twisty-turny hunk of rope with no discussion, no time for second thoughts, no hesitation. We did what we were ordered to do and to do it fast. We didn't question the lieutenant or the crew chief.

We knew that if anyone hesitated or balked, he would be pushed out the end of the open bay, or that was what our training had instilled in us. That is army discipline!

When given an order, you move and you move now! No hesitation, no thoughts, just response. The army tears you down and builds you up. You are trained to respond immediately, whether it is climbing down a ladder, forging a rapid river, climbing a rope, or charging the enemy with incoming hostile fire. And, if so ordered, you stand at attention, eyes front, in 30-degree weather for endless minutes.

We all made it—no casualties. We were now becoming disciplined and trained fighters. In eight weeks the U.S. Army had taken us from raw, wet-behind-the-ear recruits to hardened, disciplined, and toughened soldiers. We were about ready to graduate, but the real training was about to begin—we just did not know it.

POTASSIUM NITRATE

O ne often hears about GIs complaining about army chow, but most of us never did. Oh, there were the usual complaints about the Sunday supper of liver and onions, which most of us did not care for, but the quality and taste of the other meals was rather good, C-rations notwithstanding.

I guess that the navy's submariners and the army's combat-ready trained killers get the best chow. Unlike many military complexes that serve a thousand men in a giant mess hall, each company (164 men) had its own mess hall and its own cooks. Although cooking for that many guys was a task, these guys were part of our unit, so they took special care to please us.

Even though we lined up for meals, the cooks would make our breakfast eggs to order (over easy, sunny side up, or scrambled—"Wreck 'em"). If we wanted three pieces of bacon instead of two, we would get it. We sat four to a table (after the first four weeks of basic), and we had table coverings. We could have all the milk (white or chocolate) and all the food we wanted, but very seldom did anyone go back for seconds. You see, somehow we magically all consumed pretty much the same number of calories. The army's regimented approach molded everyone into a pre-established physique.

You would think that after weeks of military isolation and training, we would be love-starved for some special care and attention in the nearby town, but the army had that covered. The cooks were under orders to add saltpeter (potassium nitrate) to the food in order to suppress the GI's normal sex drive.

We graduated as trained soldiers during a dignified military ceremony held on the division's parade grounds. Although we were soldiers, we were not yet combat ready. That would come in phase two, another ten weeks of much-more intense training. First, we were granted a two-week leave, and since the airlines were on strike, I had to take a train to California and back to Kansas.

The time went by too quickly. I didn't have the time to do and see the many things I wanted. I did, however, get to experience the vastness of our great country, and I enjoyed the scenic ride.

MY MENTOR

Joe Zukin, Jr., my mentor and president of Frontier Village Amusement Park, was in the same brigade (39th) during World War II. Joe was a platoon leader, a 2nd lieutenant stationed in Germany. After graduating high school in June 1943 at age seventeen, he started at Stanford University in Palo Alto, majoring in business administration. The war was going full bore, and at the end of his freshman year, Joe enlisted in the army. He had wanted to join the army air corps and fly, but color blindness kept him out of that branch. The army quickly saw that they had a bright, intelligent, and dedicated soldier in Joe, and so they shipped him off to OCS (officer candidate school) to become a 2nd lieutenant in the infantry. His one-hundred-day basic training was at Camp Roberts in California; while his ninety-day wonder (officer) training was at Fort Benning, Georgia.

Having scored extremely high on the AFQT (Armed Forces Qualification Test), he was assigned to intelligence operations but trained as an infantry officer. He was well versed in the tactics and weapons of infantry fighting and was ready to fight the Germans. He graduated in June 1945, but by then the war in Europe had ended. Joe hoped to be shipped to the South Pacific to fight, but the army had other ideas for this rising star. He was assigned as an instructor at Camp Robinson, Arkansas, teaching young recruits the fine art of using the Browning Automatic Rifle (BAR) and bayonet tactics.

After four months as a training officer, Lieutenant Joseph Zukin, Jr., was sent to the 9th Infantry Division in Germany in September 1945 and assigned to the 39th Infantry Brigade, 3rd Battalion, Headquarters Company. He had the delicate task of helping to relocate displaced persons back to their countries of origin. The Germans had taken people from their captured lands and put them to war work in Germany. The U.S. Army had the task of relocation of millions of these people. Joe coordinated the assembly, transportation, care, and movement of thousands of refugees via train, back to various countries. He had a golden opportunity to visit many parts of Germany and neighboring countries, and carried

18

on with his assignment until shipping back to the states in September 1946. The army tried to keep Joe, but he wanted to finish his education at Stanford, which he did, and then he started his life as an entrepreneur.

Joe loved the service and had given thought to making it career, but many of us employees who worked for him were happy that he decided to build Frontier Village, thus creating lifelong careers for many of his hardworking employees. During my leave, Joe presented me with an Octofoil (sunflower) shoulder patch that he had worn while serving as a 2nd lieutenant with the 9th Infantry Division, 39th Brigade in Germany during World War II. I wore it proudly as I slugged through the muck and steaming heat of the Vietnamese jungles; the stately tall trees of the rubber (Michelin Tire) plantations; the high, thick grass of the Iron Triangle; the watery and putrid-smelling mangrove swamps in the Mekong Delta; and the mountainous and "cold" (70 degrees) Pleiku highlands.

I still have that special shoulder patch, although it is somewhat torn and tattered. Combat-hardened GIs receive special uniform recognition not afforded other military units. Those who serve in a combat unit are permitted to wear their combat unit shoulder patch on their uniform in addition to their unit's current patch. You will not see many soldiers with two unit shoulder patches. Only one in eleven soldiers is in a combat unit (infantry, armor, or artillery), and very few of those ever experience actual combat conditions. More on that later, when I tell you the Combat Infantry Badge (CIB) story.

Thank you, Joe. That patch holds a very special meaning for me.

NOW THE FUN BEGINS

As I boarded the train in San Jose for the trip back to Kansas at the end of my leave, I wondered what new things the army had up its sleeve for me. As we all gathered back at Charlie Company, we were different soldiers. Yes, we were trained, physically fit, and somewhat hardened, but we were still naive about the art of combat. We had been trained to kill, and mentally we could do that, but impressing it upon our psyche was the next step. Here is where the ten weeks of AIT, advanced individual training, would harden us individually and bring us together as a cohesive unit. We would become a unified killing machine.

Advanced individual training is just that—advanced, specialized training for each individual in a select combat discipline. Some guys temporarily left the unit to train as medics or in radio communications, mortar and machine gun (M-60[1]), or other specialties. Others became explosives and booby-trap experts. A couple of small fellas went to "tunnel rat" school, and they proved to be very good at their jobs as we discovered in the thick jungle environment.

Four of us in the platoon had specialized training in combat leadership—how to lead men under fire and have them perform impossible feats under very demanding conditions. Wow—I learned the army's success secrets, the power of effective leadership, and a lot about myself. At age twenty-two I was sucking it all in. I was good fodder for the army's special development program. They filled my head with mind-expanding concepts. In the leadership classes we learned land navigation (map and compass). Did you know the three types of "north"? True, grid, and magnetic. Calling in artillery fire, explosives, and marking rounds[2] was an important skill that later came in handy—especially those marking rounds. Willy Peter—white phosphorus—is

---

1 The M-60 machine gun is a .30 caliber weapon. M-60s were carried by us (weapons squad) in each platoon. Door gunners on the UH-1D assault helicopters also used them. The bandoleers of bullets you see each soldier carrying are the .30 caliber rounds for the M-60 machine gun. The .50 caliber machine guns used on tanks used larger and heavier rounds.

2 A marking round is a smoke-filled artillery shell, which is fired in advance of an explosive round to help mark the exact coordinates of the target before the firing of the actual live explosive.

20

hot, nasty stuff. We were taught ambush tactics, search-and-destroy procedures, explosive and demolition tactics, radio procedures, and a little bit of the Vietnamese language, which came in quite handy. We learned a smattering of other combat skills, and got shots—lots and lots of shots.

ARMOR, RIVERS, AND HUEYS

After we completed AIT, we spent another couple of months training as a unit (company, battalion, and division). Here we practiced, as if in real combat situations, helicopter, armor, and patrol-training maneuvers for countless hours. We crossed rivers, both on foot and in armored personnel carriers (APCs), and we flew in helicopters to attack "enemy" strongholds.

We were in the field day and night, attacking, setting up bivouacs, and blowing up tunnels and fortifications. We had plenty of live-fire (rifle, artillery, and mortar) exercises. Those 88s, 105s, and 155 guns are loud! Night search-and-destroy missions and ambushes became the norm for us.

This training was more exhausting and demanding than basic training had been. We were in the field literally the entire ten weeks. The training simulated the conditions and situations we would soon be facing in the jungles, swamps, and villages of Southeast Asia.

At this time, we really came together as units, and we came to understand each other's true strengths and weaknesses. It may be a little egotistic, but we were a tough unit. No, certainly not battle hardened; that would come in another four months during Operation Cedar Falls, but we were certainly ready for the tasks that awaited us. We truly did think, act, and perform differently than when it had all begun seven months earlier.

Toward the end of our AIT training in fall 1966, it was turning cold on the flat plains of Kansas. The guys with whom I had trained for the previous six months were now becoming a combat-ready unit.

After training, we had two weeks leave, but it was a more somber time. This was it. We were not informed that we would be shipping off to Vietnam, but nobody imagined otherwise. After all, we had trained as a division, and our motto was "Anything, Anytime, Anywhere, Bar None!"

Ours was a long and proud history to uphold, and we were ready for the task. The 9th Division was a well-oiled, combat-ready, fighting division. Even the press was now reporting on our hard and special training. Mom later wrote me that she and Dad had seen a news clip on TV about our preparation and impending departure. The Vietnam War was raging, and the whole country was watching this new "television" war.

The 9th Infantry Division was one crack and tough unit. I know that that might sound conceited, but the reader needs to remember that the Vietnam War was the biggest military conflict since World War II. The military was training us to go in and fight the VC. They had given us the best officers, equipment, training, and support. We were going to do battle with a Communist aggressor.

PACKING IT UP

Upon returning to Fort Riley, Camp Forsyth, we started to literally break camp. We had just a couple of weeks to pack up everything within the company and battalion compounds and get it on a train and then to a ship docked in Oakland, California. We spent the next twelve days like busy ants getting ready for winter. Each man was assigned to a detail. Some guys built containers and crates, others packed items, and others did the heavy lifting of things onto flatbeds and deuce-and-a-halfs, while others rode with the loads to railcars on base. We packed up everything. The mess hall, barracks, company and battalion head-quarters equipment, ammunition, vehicles, and supplies. If it was not nailed down, it got packed up. A caravan of deuce-and-a-halfs and flat-bed trucks went back and forth to the rail yard. I saw flatcars loaded with tanks, helicopters, and armored personnel carriers. As a squad leader (of ten guys), my task was to supervise the squad in a variety of tasks. Primarily, squad leaders rode the trucks to the rail yard and unloaded the materials into the waiting boxcars. Back and forth we went, day after day, escorting the loaded trucks from battalion grounds to freight cars.

I had learned early on in my military days that the best position to be in was one of leadership and supervision. I did not want to do physical work (K.P. or kitchen police, cleaning latrines, or cutting the colonel's lawn) but rather to oversee the work of others. Although supervision takes a certain knack, I had the skill set to be successful. (Thank you, Joe Zukin and Frontier Village.) Motivating others to be productive was much better than bending your own back. Supervising the transportation and transfer of materials was right up my supervision alley. Although the hours were long, it was not hard duty for me. My squad respected me, as also proved to be the case in the jungles of Vietnam, and we got along fairly well— as well as can be expected under hostile conditions.

We worked twelve-hour days getting things ready for rail shipment, a massive effort. A whole division was loading up and heading west. Nothing like this had been done since World War II, some twenty-six years earlier. We did not know it at the time, but the freight trains were taking our gear to the waiting ship, the USNS *General Alexander M. Patch*, at the Port of Oakland, and all our gear was being loaded onto the ship, which would await our arrival a few days later. The only things not being shipped at that moment were the clothes we were wearing, our stuffed duffle bags, and our trusty M-16 rifles, which we carried with us twenty-four hours a day. We spent most of those two weeks living with our combat gear and eating C-rations. We were permitted to use the toilets in one barracks and sleep on the barracks floor, but that was it. No showers, no change of clothes, just bare-bones existence. This was our final toughening-up exercise.

On the last day we nailed up the barracks windows, turned off the lights, and waited for that 1:00 A.M. final call. Of course, all leaves (liberty) were cancelled during those two weeks, and we were restricted to the company compound. We did not even get mail, nor could we send it. The MPs (Military Police) were constantly patrolling the area around the company and battalion grounds. You would have thought we were going off to war. We were.

LET'S GET THIS SHOW ON THE ROAD!

Then, one cold morning at 1:30 A.M., we were awakened and given thirty minutes to get ready to move out. This was in late November; it may have been around Thanksgiving, but by then we had lost all track of time. We did not know the month or day. Our focus had been on the mission of packing up, and the days and nights had run together. We grabbed our duffle bags, which were stacked by the barracks door, and with our M-16s slung over our shoulders, we fell into formation one last time. We were leaving what had been our home for the previous seven months. I can still remember the smell of diesel fumes and wet canvas tarps as we boarded the trucks. Twenty guys, bunched up on wooden seats, rifles between their legs, and alone with their private thoughts. Not many talked; the show was about to begin.

Our seven months of intense training was about to make its showing. We were trained killers—truly God's Lunatics. Like it or not, we knew how to kill in hand-to-hand encounters, with knives and bayonets, with small arms (M-16s), explosives, plastic explosives, C-4, Claymore mines, hand grenades, and artillery firepower. How would we react under actual combat conditions? We would be tested individually and as a unit. Would our training match the actual conditions we would be facing? Uncle Sam had poured hundreds of thousands of dollars into each man to make him a killing machine. Back in the 1960s, that was a lot of money, time, and effort for such an undertaking. Today we have the Black Ops, Navy Seals, Special Forces, Rangers, and many other specialized killing and combat units, but back then it was a new, specialized type of warfare. Many times we were small units, working alone, fighting an often elusive and slippery enemy. We had to be prepared to stand alone if air, artillery, or armor support was not available, which we discovered was the reality, deep in the thick, mapless jungle.

Riding in the back of a rumbling, cold, damp deuce-and-a-half was not new to us. We had spent countless hours being transported to and from field classes and exercises, but somehow this time it seemed different. It was more like our final ride to destiny—whatever that might be for each of us. We were bouncing down the dark roads of dew-covered Kansas flatlands, leaving behind the sweat and toil of our individual and joint efforts. Now we were on our way to a troop train and ship that would deliver us to the land of milk and honey. (Yeah, right!) Second Brigade had been shipped to Vietnam by air transports, but First Brigade had the distinction of making a twenty-one-day ocean voyage aboard the USNS *General Alexander M. Patch,* a troop transport ship. Now that was a real adventure with 5,000 stinky guys.

At the train depot, there were no Red Cross ladies with coffee, donuts, or hot chocolate. No band was playing; no goodbye and good luck speeches. It was cold, dark, and clandestine. The long string of army troop cars sat cold and stark in the clear, crisp, autumn night. Occasionally a lone hiss came out of a steam air brake, but that was it. It was a solemn and quiet send-off. The officers hustled us off the trucks, formed us into platoons, and instructed us to file silently into the waiting 1950s-vintage train cars. Each platoon had been assigned a specific section, and with military precision, we threw our duffle bags into the undercarriage storage areas and boarded the train, each one carrying his M-16 or machine gun. It was evident that the officers had practiced this routine. There was no confusion or question as to which unit went where. It was a swift and orchestrated transfer from truck to train. Yep, even the windows were blacked out. This was a hush-hush maneuver. I guess they did not want the VC (Viet Cong) to know that we were on our way.

Within a half hour, the train was moving west. We were not told where we were headed, but three and a half days later we pulled into the army depot in Oakland, where it had all started for me. While on the blacked-out train ride, we did get to use the lone shower in each car. We lined up to eat in the nice dining car on white linen tablecloths and to use the lone toilet in each car. We didn't have much to do except read, play cards, and sleep. We certainly had no scenery to watch. Day and night, the train rolled on.

ANCHORS AWEIGH

The train pulled up next to a large, waiting troop transport ship, the USNS *General Alexander M. Patch*, named after an army general. Wow, what valet service. I was wondering if some nice officers would unload and carry our duffle bags up the gangplank for us, but no such luck. The old army motto of "hurry up and wait" certainly did not apply to our loading and unloading from the train, however. Within fifteen minutes we were off the train and formed up into our platoons. We gathered our duffle bags and climbed the steep gangplank onto this 5,000-person troop ship. Just like in the movies, we climbed down ladders deep into the bowels of the ship, well below the waterline. Each platoon was assigned a bunking section, and we each took one of the bunks, which were stacked six high with eighteen inches between. We stowed our duffle bags in sections along the sloping inside wall of the ship. Each bunk had a thin mattress, and, just like on the train, we were going to be sleeping in our fatigues. We were crammed in like sardines—row after row of GIs on thousands of bunk beds. This would be our quarters for the next twenty-one days! We did not realize it then, but sleeping in the hot, wet jungle would be much nicer than these quarters. The GIs assigned to fly to Vietnam had it a lot nicer. After having been cooped up on the train for three days, the ship did afford us more freedom. At least we could do some moving around during the day.

We sailed at 8:00 A.M. the next cold and grey day. Soldiers who could were on the ship's deck to watch our departure. For the next twenty-one days we were in the Pacific Ocean, heading southwest toward hot and humid Vietnam. As we moved toward the South Pacific, the weather became warmer and more humid. As we crossed the equator, we found the meager air conditioning in the sleeping areas did little to alleviate the stink, sweat, and humidity of thousands of GIs cramped into the tight quarters. It was like the hot hell we would soon encounter in the jungle. Ah, another real-life training experience. There was not much to do aboard ship, as space was limited, except to line up for everything—chow, showers (salt water every fourth day —salt water was used as to conserve fresh, potable water), latrines, and daily exercise. We slept on deck, watched the endless ocean roll by, or perhaps read the small bibles handed out by the chaplain. The ocean is beautiful and moody. It takes on various colors, temperaments, and expressions. And the stars—tons of stars. On a blackened-out ship and in the lightless Pacific, so many stars filled the nighttime sky. Much of the trip was calm sailing, but many guys got seasick the first few days. I was fortunate and enjoyed the gentle rolling. Sea travel suited me just fine, and the salt air did heighten my appetite.

As late November rolled into December 1966, the weather turned warmer as we moved past Hawaii and into the South Pacific. It was becoming humid, and we were becoming acclimated to the heat. Somewhere near Vietnam we encountered a tropical storm. Although we were not in its direct path, we were told we would skirt it. While we were eating evening chow, a big swell rolled through an open porthole and drenched us, our food, and made a mess—the first of many unexpected surprises that awaited us during the next twelve months.

Our trip took three weeks of sailing (we had had turkey for Christmas dinner while on the high seas) and six days of sitting in Vung Tau Harbor, Vietnam. As we waited in the harbor, the anchored ship would drift with the tides. I had learned about that in school, but to actually experience it was interesting. I would go to sleep with the ship facing land, and the next morning it would be seaward. The waiting to disembark was the most boring time. We experienced a number of false starts, but that was probably planned just to keep us occupied—the old hurry-up-and-wait routine. Finally, one day (the 29th of December, I believe), we lined up at the railing in full gear with duffle bags at our feet as the landing craft began to arrive. Welcome to Vietnam. The long, slow disembarking process began.

WELCOME TO VIETNAM

Yes, just like the movies, we disembarked the USNS *General Alexander M. Patch* by climbing down the side of the great ship on rope ladders. We had practiced climbing down rope ladders in basic, but that was on dry land with the ladder hanging next to a stable wooden wall. Here we were, in a safe harbor, but the tide was running, the ladder was swaying, and the landing crafts were bobbing. Before starting the climb over the railing—in full combat gear—we had to throw our duffle bag over the side to another waiting craft, which carried them to shore ahead of us. As we climbed down, rung-by-rung, we swayed back and forth. A couple guys lost their helmets, and one guy dropped his M-16 into the harbor, but we all made it—some 5,000 of us—without a serious injury.

It was a short ride, maybe ten minutes, from the ship to the landing beach where the craft dropped its ramp. Seventy-five or so new combat soldiers waded ashore and quickly climbed aboard deuce-and-a-halfs for the ride to Camp Bearcat, the home of the 9th Infantry Division, some fifty miles north. As the trucks moved along dirt roads, children and villagers came out to await the GIs, who tossed them candy, cigarettes, and C-rations. Hey, we were greenhorns, fair skinned, and ready to fight the VC (Viet Cong—*Victor Charlie*, in radio talk) in the thick, steaming jungles. We would soon be learning some hard and lasting lessons about life, the enemy, and ourselves. We were about to grow up fast. We would soon become bloodied and muddied!

The 9th Infantry Division had the dual honor of being the first division since World War II reactivated for direct deployment into combat and the last division sent to Vietnam. The Division had received its colors at Fort Riley, Kansas, on February 1, 1966. Division engineering elements began arriving in Vietnam during October 1966. The first 5,000-troop contingent landed on the beaches of Vinh Long on December 19, 1966. Division headquarters was at Camp Bearcat (formerly Camp Martin Cox) some 20 miles northeast of Saigon.

Camp Bearcat was still under construction when we arrived. We were the second of four brigades (*regiments* in World War II) to arrive, but our battalion section was up and ready. The 9th had been assigned to III Corps' field of operation—from the Mekong Delta in the south to the highlands of Plieku. From mangrove swamps to tall elephant grass (it is as tall as an elephant) in the Iron Triangle. We would do battle in every type of terrain—steaming jungles, stagnant swamps, rice paddies, elephant grass, and high mountain areas. From 22 degrees on the plains of Kansas to 112 degrees and 100 percent humidity in the jungles of Southeast Asia.

It was called Camp Bearcat because a bearcat signifies something with exceptional power, strength, and energy. That was us, the Old Reliables.

BRINGING IN THE 9TH

I t was reported that the bloodiest six months of the Vietnam War occurred during spring and summer 1967. No argument here. The war
was at its height, President Johnson and General Westmoreland inserted
570,000 troops into the heart of Vietnam, but only 60,000 were actual
fighting troops (infantry, armor, artillery, and combat aircraft). One major offensive was put on hold awaiting the arrival of the well-trained,
15,000 strong, 9th Infantry Division.

Yes, the 9th would play a major role in the Cedar Falls and Junction
City (named after the town next to Fort Riley in Kansas) operations. The
39th Infantry (Brigade), as we would experience, would be in the thick
of it.

BASIC LOAD

Not *long ago, Jim Haines, a fellow Vietnam vet who was in the 9th with me, contacted me. Jim has been organizing vet reunions for many years. I showed him a draft of my remembrances, and he said that it was like walking in my boots. Jim, who was in Bravo Company, was kind enough to write up his recollection of what the basic "jungle killer" carried into battle. I am presenting here Jim's exact recollection of that topic, which, I believe, will be helpful to all readers.*

(Sgt.) Warren P. Weitzel

Vietnam—1967

From Jim Haines:

"Most of the army operations of Mobile Riverine Force lasted three to five days. We would be resupplied once a day by helicopter or boat, so if we needed it during the day, we had to carry it with us. When immersion foot [a.k.a. trench foot] and ring worm set in, they took us out to let our feet dry out.

Whenever a grunt goes out to the field, he has to carry whatever he needs for a day with him. The unit's needs are dispersed within the unit. For that reason every man is assigned a basic load that consists of his personal weapon and ammo, hand grenades, and ammo for the machine gun. Weapons like Claymores and M-72s were assigned to one guy per fire team. Each squad also had to carry a grappling hook, an extra barrel for the machine gun, a radio, an extra battery for the radio, rope, and explosives. One guy in each platoon got a Starlight scope and another guy got a shotgun to carry, too. Everybody got something.

The rest of the load consisted of food, water, cleaning equipment for your weapon, knives, machetes, poncho, etc. It also included the rucksack and web gear to carry it all on, and that damn steel helmet, too!

The area of operation determined some of the load, too. For example, if it was in a known booby-trapped area, a flak jacket would be necessary. Each squad would bring an air mattress or two on which to float equipment across any big rivers. Just more stuff to carry with us.

The basic load of ammunition for an M-16 was twenty magazines at about a pound apiece, and 200 rounds on stripper clips, about twenty-five pounds total. The basic load for an M-79 grenade launcher was twenty rounds of high explosive and five beehive rounds. (A beehive round is an anti-personnel shell filled with tiny metal darts, which are ejected from the shell during flight. It is so called because of the buzzing sound the darts make when flying through the air.) The grenadier also carried a .45 caliber automatic pistol with four magazines. That added up to about thirty-five pounds. The M-60 machine gunner carried two one-hundred-round belts of ammo, a twenty-five-round belt of tracers, and a twenty-five-round belt in the gun. The M-60 was the heaviest weapon, and its firepower was important enough that everyone carried ammo for it.

We knew how to figure out how much weight to assign a guy. We just kept piling it on until he could not move any more. It took some time to determine the best load and the best way for each individual could carry it. I had more than I could carry at first. With the help of some of the older guys, we found the best weight for me and the best way to carry it. I was a skinny white boy who, although in the best shape of my life, could not carry as much as some of the other guys.

This is what my load consisted of:

One M-16 rifle
Nineteen magazines of M-16 ammo (eighteen rounds each)
One magazine of M-16 tracer ammo (eighteen rounds each)
200 Rounds of M-16 ammo on stripper clips
Four fragmentation grenades
Two smoke grenades
Two one-hundred-round belts of M-60 ammo
One grappling hook and fifty feet of rope
One machete with scabbard
One gas mask with case
One field dressing with pouch
One steel helmet with liner
One aluminum rucksack with shoulder straps
One pistol belt
Two ammo pouches
One poncho

Three C-ration meals
Four canteens of water
Two four-ounce bottles of insect repellant
Four packs of cigarettes
One M-16 cleaning rod
One shaving brush
One toothbrush (for cleaning weapons)
One toothbrush (for cleaning teeth)
One can of tooth powder
One layer of Mekong Delta mud

However, as time went on, I was able to manage the load better. I added a net hammock, a poncho liner, and a pair of socks; they added an M-72 LAW (light antitank weapon). After a while, I no longer had the M-72, but I got a Starlight scope (night vision scope that relies on ambient light instead of an infrared light). Then I got rid of the grappling hook to a new guy and got a Claymore mine. With a few other changes here and there, that was my load for my first five months in country. Then I became a radio operator. Subtract Claymores and Starlight scope from the above list and add a radio.

The PRC-25 radio was built to survive. It had to be. It was a box about the same size as a baby AT computer case, and it weighed twenty-five pounds. Army and navy used it. It could be mounted in a vehicle, set on a desk in an operations center, or carried on a rucksack. It was a good load by itself, but add to it most of the stuff from the list above and you have more load than a pack mule should have to carry.

Radio operators were preferred targets, so most of us attempted to camouflage it. We bent the flexible antenna down through a ring on the front of the shoulder strap so it would not stick up like a flagpole. I liked to break up the sight line by hanging a machete on the right side and C-rations rolled up in a poncho on the back. On the left side, I strapped a segmented long whip antenna wrapped in an olive-drab towel and a sock filled with rice for cooking. It was a good, tightly strapped, well-positioned arrangement. It was a heavier load than before, but it was more manageable than the old collection of stuff.

Carrying that load through mud and mangrove swamps and jumping canals and crossing rivers with it can leave you with raw shoulders and an aching back. However, that is what the job required. That is why when I see a war movie and they are wearing only a pistol belt with a canteen on it, I laugh. Can't they get actors to carry some weight?"

—*Jim Haines*

HITTING THE JUNGLE RUNNING

The army wanted to get a quick return on the big bucks they had spent training the 9th. We had a day or two to get "settled" into our base camp for all the good it would do us. Of the year "in-country," we probably spent only eighteen to twenty days at Bearcat. We were a disciplined fighting unit, and that is what we did—we fought in the jungles, swamps, and grasslands. This was not a pleasure tour. We were there to do a job, and by God, the 9th was going to do it.

We did basic patrols outside the base camp area during the first couple of weeks. Construction was going on, and the base was expanding. Rome plows[3] were clearing away the jungle, and more barracks and buildings were being erected. Sometimes we would be assigned to ride shotgun on the dozers as they pushed back the jungle. We would perch on some small spot on the dozer and watch the trees for snipers. Occasionally we would encounter a booby trap or a sniper, but nothing big. I got shot at once but never saw from where it came, and I didn't return fire—that time. The sniper had taken a bead on the dozer I was guarding. I did not see or hear where the sniper had shot from, but the driver and I both heard two rounds hit the engine covering and ricochet. He kept cutting down trees, and I kept looking around in the trees for Charlie. (Charlie probably was not in the trees but at ground level, moving back as the jungle clearing encroached on his domain.) We learned that this sniping activity was not unusual. However, even the periodic patrols into the surrounding jungle did not dissuade the snipers.

Soon we were riding shotgun on truck convoys as they moved men and materials from the port of Vung Tau or an airbase. On one run, the driver, a pimply-faced kid said to me, "You guys [infantry] don't talk much."

---

3 Rome plows were large, armored, specially modified bulldozers used in South Vietnam by the United States military during the Vietnam War to clear jungle vegetation, thus removing cover that could be used by the Viet Cong and North Vietnamese forces. The plows take their name from the city of Rome, Georgia, where they were made by the Rome Plow Company (now located in Cedartown, Georgia). The plows were equipped with a very sharp two-ton "stinger" blade that could cut down trees, which were then burned. When fully equipped, a Rome plow weighed at least 36,000 pounds. —Wikipedia

"Nope," I said, "We're not the talking type. We don't want to get to know someone too well. He might get killed, and we'd feel real bad."

He said nothing else during the long drive. It was not like the long dialogue scene between Bubba and Forrest Gump in the movie.

After a month of light "babysitting" duty, we graduated to more-serious business. We had a couple of weeklong search-and-destroy operations involving dozer-infantry teams. Things were beginning to get hot, both in temperature and enemy contact.

THEM'S BULLETS!

On one occasion, we were helicoptered out a distance to assist an engineer battalion in clearing an area. We provided support for about a day and then received orders to search a nearby village and surrounding jungle for suspected VC strongholds. This day, this incident vividly sticks in my mind, for it was one of those significant emotional encounters that are often life-altering moments. It was our first significant firefight and it occurred roughly sixty days after arriving in Vietnam. Our platoon (forty-two guys) was walking through a rice paddy, approaching a village. Some of us were walking atop the narrow berms, while others were sloshing through the water-filled paddies. All of a sudden, from the village, it happened—machine gun fire. Our first enemy contact!

Yikes! The training kicked in. As it so happened, I had the lead squad, and the lieutenant yelled for me to move my squad to the right flank position, some fifty meters. As I began running, I heard another burst of machine gun fire coming from the village. I looked down at the top of the dike and saw little puffs of dirt being kicked up. My world seemed to S-L-O-W D-O-W-N

Them's bullets! I thought to myself, and I kept running. When I reached a clump of trees, I took cover and immediately started shaking all over. Those bastards were shooting at me, trying to kill me. What seemed like a minute of fear was probably only a few seconds, and then it kicked in. Nobody's going to shoot at me and get away with it. I instinctively raised my M-16 and fired away, emptying the twenty-round clip.

As I reloaded, I signaled the rest of the squad to direct fire toward the hooch (Vietnamese hut) from which we thought the machine gun was firing. The training worked. All those sergeants and officers yelling at us had taken away any fear. The adrenalin took hold, and we were now truly a fighting unit. Every man did his job. We had taken up good field-of-fire positions and were covering the other squads, who were by then heavy into the fighting.

Bullets were zinging through the air all over the place. This was combat! Our machine gunner had set up for action and was burning smoke from the M-60 barrel. We were starting to pass our bandoleers of machine gun bullets to the gunner. One or two guys would gather up the rounds and run them to the location while the rest of us laid down heavy cover fire.

The lieutenant was directing us to move to various positions, just as we had done in training. We did not want to stay in one spot too long or the enemy would zero in on us. Move, fire, move, fire, and keep advancing on the enemy. One squad got into position; their grenadier (M-79) launched a couple of grenades into the hooch of the suspected machine-gun nest. The firing stopped suddenly. We cautiously moved up to the hooch, and a couple of guys entered it from the rear. One VC was dead, and the other pretty badly wounded.

All of us, including the lieutenant, were on an adrenalin high—our first firefight! Score one for us. The lieutenant calmed us down and had us set up a perimeter. We searched the village. The dead VC was loaded onto a poncho for transport back to the LZ (helicopter landing zone). His partner had his hands tied, and one squad took the prisoner and body back to the LZ for pickup. (The rumor was that the prisoner did not make it back to the base camp. Had he been "double tapped"?)

It took us a while to come down from the rush. For the next few hours we congratulated each other and embellished our "war stories." As the day wore on, we got back to our disciplined routine but still stood tall; we had individually and as a unit performed well under actual combat conditions.

For the next few days, as we searched our way back to Camp Bearcat, we were focused and sharp. Upon arrival, the camp was buzzing about our "big firefight." We were the first platoon to be in a confirmed combatant action against a hostile force. This made us proud, and of course, Lieutenant Leslie was making his military mark.

In a company ceremony, attended by the battalion lieutenant colonel, we received our coveted Combat Infantry Badges (CIB). Well, not the actual badge, but a combat patch that we proudly sewed onto our battle fatigues.

"War is a violent teacher." – Thucydides

COMBAT IS MUCH LIKE FOOTBALL

Combat training is an art. People often view a battle scene as a bunch of guys shooting at each other, when in reality it is a battle of wits as much as ammunition. Fans will view a football game as two opposing teams lining up and, when the ball is snapped, scrambling and fighting to advance or take control of the ball. That is true, and the entire team's focus is on doing just that, but underneath the scramble for ball control is an orchestrated movement of eleven different guys, each trained in a slightly different discipline (tackle, guard, tight end, wide receiver, fullback) designed to enhance the ball control. The coach and quarterback are the off- and on-field coordinators of this subtle but important activity of ball control and movement.

Combat is very much like a scrimmage in football. Each squad of ten combat infantrymen is trained to engage, close with, and kill the enemy. That is the basic purpose, but within each squad are guys with specialized skills, such as riflemen, grenadiers, tunnel rats, explosives, ropes and scaling, and the "quarterback" sergeant. Sure, each soldier can do each other's job, but each guy is an expert in his trained discipline.

The lieutenant is the coach, and although not on the sidelines, he calls the plays. In his mind, he has a battle plan for moving the squads of men toward an objective and taking it. To close with and kill the enemy—to control the ball. The lieutenant, through his four-squad leaders, will skillfully and systematically engage the enemy through a series of programmed movements and actions. It may appear to be a bunch of lunatics running, shooting, and killing, but underneath is a finely trained lieutenant who is hopefully five chess moves ahead of the opponent. Our lives depended on his tactical thinking and deployment skills, and it was our job to protect him and kill the enemy.

41

AN ARMY INFANTRY LESSON

It is a misconception that everyone in the military is in a combat unit. Everyone goes through some sort of basic training, but upon graduation, many go into specialized units, including maintenance, personnel, medical, transportation, quartermaster, logistics, communications, and many more. These people may never hold a rifle or be only remotely involved with combatant disciplines after basic training. For every one person in a combat unit (infantry, artillery, and armor—tanks), eleven more play some sort of support role. Only a small percentage of soldiers—even in times of war, such as Vietnam—ever see any sort of combat. Of the 570,000 troops in Vietnam at the height of the Vietnam War in 1967, only 60,000 were in combat units. Even units such as artillery may be removed from the front lines and may never face enemy fire.

Combat units (infantry, armor, and artillery) do get special recognition on their uniform. In the army, such unit personnel will wear color-identifying ascots (light blue for infantry, yellow for armor, and red for artillery) to identify them as combat soldiers. In addition, the infantry soldier who has seen actual combat (thirty or more days of engagement with a hostile force) will proudly wear the Combat Infantry Badge. Ribbons and awards are worn on the dress uniform (Class A or B) in the ranking from the lowest award or decoration on the bottom to the highest on the top. This colorful array of ribbons is called "fruit salad." You will always see the CIB worn on the very top of the collection of ribbons.

COMBAT INFANTRY BADGE (CIB)

The infantry's primary mission, its training and focus, is to "close with and destroy the enemy." No questions asked, no ambiguity, no grey areas.

The Combat Infantry Badge (CIB) is awarded to the wartime infantryman, the soldier who generally suffers the worst privations. The recipient must be an infantry or Special Forces soldier who performs satisfactorily in a unit engaged in combat. Soldiers in field uniform (Class C—fatigues) are permitted to wear only four forms of identification besides their name, rank, and unit patch. (Remember that those who have been in actual combat may also wear their combat unit patch in addition to their regular unit patch.) The Pathfinder insignia, Ranger tab, Airborne wings, or Combat Infantry Badge are the only other four insignia that may be worn on one's fatigues. Great respect is given to soldiers wearing any of these. It shows that they have paid their combat dues. There is no cockier soldier than the one wearing the Airborne wings, Ranger tab, or CIB.

SPECIAL RESPECT AT FORT SILL, OKLAHOMA

Jumping ahead a little bit, after returning from Vietnam, I was temporarily assigned to Headquarters Company, 4th Army, at Fort Sill, Oklahoma. (I will tell you more about this soft duty a little later.) Enlisted men always salute officers, and officers then return the salute. The lower-ranking soldier always initiates the salute to the higher rank and holds it until it is returned.

In headquarters company, we were sharp dressers, and I wore starched fatigues and my CIB patch. Soon after my arrival, I noticed that the officers would initiate the salute to me before I started to salute them. I thought that was odd. About my second day at Fort Sill, I was standing in the chow line at breakfast, and one of the men asked me what I was doing.

"I'm waiting for chow," was my snappy reply.

"No," he said. "Why aren't you at the head of the line? You know, guys like you get special privileges."

"What do you mean?"

"The colonel has mandated that all CIB recipients are to be saluted by officers, and you guys get to eat either in the officers' mess hall or go to the front of the line in the enlisted men's mess hall."

That was news to me, but I liked the special recognition. After eating cold C-rations and sloshing through muck and fighting leeches, this sounded pretty good. It seemed that the colonel had a special fondness for the combat soldier and had given a directive for special treatment and recognition. I later learned that there were only seventeen CIB recipients in our battalion, and that was the colonel's way of showing his appreciation.

Getting to move to the head of the chow line was a real perk. Not only did I not have to wait, but the cooks also gave us extra attention and extra chow. I liked the four pieces of bacon instead of the allotted two. I managed to pack on a few extra pounds during those four soft-duty months. Even the guys working the mess hall would get me an extra glass of chocolate milk from the Norris machine. Life was sweet.

As we will talk about later, working in the personnel section was the softest duty a combat-hardened buck sergeant could have.

VETERANS DAY

Memorial Day, in May, is in honor of our fallen war veterans, and Veterans Day, in November, honors our living war veterans. The soldier is the army. No army is better than its soldiers. The soldier is also a citizen. In fact, the highest obligation and privilege of citizenship is that of bearing arms for one's country. Hence, it is a proud privilege to be a soldier, a good soldier. Anyone in any walk of life who is content with mediocrity is untrue to himself or herself and to American tradition. To be a good soldier, a man must have discipline, self-respect, pride in his unit and in his country, a high sense of duty and obligation to his comrades and to his superiors, and self-confidence born of demonstrated ability.

"Self-confidence, the greatest military virtue, results from the sense of duty, discipline, and obedience, and from the exercise in the use of weapons. No sane man is unafraid in battle, but discipline produces in him a form of vicarious courage, which, with his manhood, makes for victory. Self-respect grows directly from discipline. The Army saying, 'Who ever saw a dirty soldier with a medal?' is largely true. Pride, in turn, stems from self-respect and from the knowledge that the soldier is an American. The sense of duty and obligation to his comrades and superiors comes from a knowledge of reciprocal obligation, and from the sharing of the same way of life.

"It is an unfortunate and, to me, tragic fact that in our attempts to prevent war we have taught our people to belittle the heroic qualities of the soldier. They do not realize that, as Shakespeare put it, 'The bubble reputation even at the cannon's mouth' is not only a good military characteristic but also very helpful to the young man when bullets and shells are whistling and cracking around him. Much more could be done if women of Americans would praise their heroes."

—General George S. Patton, War As I Knew It

THE BLOODIEST SIX MONTHS

The war was getting hot! Operation Junction City, the largest operation of the war, was about to begin. From the spring through fall of 1967, we saw some of the bloodiest and muddiest fighting. We did not know it at the time, but the VC were preparing for the upcoming Tet Offensive in January 1968. Our time in Vietnam was spent in the combat zones. The 9th had no base camp relaxation. We would board helicopters (UH-1Ds, or Hueys) carrying eight fully loaded combat soldiers and be shuttled to an area for deployment.

We would land in an open area, and if it was a suspected "hot" (potential enemy contact) landing zone (LZ), the choppers' door gunners would spray the area with M-60 machine gun fire. They liked doing that.

Of the several dozen landings we made, I recall only one or two actually being hot, where we actually took fire from the VC. Going into an area by helicopter was nice because we did not have to fight the terrain to get to our area of operation, but we were also vulnerable to surprise enemy contact. On a few occasions, the LZ would not be hot initially, but Charlie would wait for the choppers to depart and then surprise us with an attack. Usually it was a small force, five or seven irregular forces, and they would harass us and after a few minutes melt away into the jungle. Landing Zones were not always open and flat terrain, however. At times we would land in small, swampy areas, or jump into rice paddies, land on dusty dirt roads or even jump out from a seven- to fifteen-foot height, or so it seemed.

On one early mission, the rookie chopper pilot was skittish about landing in a dusty field, so he hovered several feet off the ground. The copilot told us to jump! We thought it was only a couple feet off the ground, but it must have been more like ten to twelve. We tumbled into a jumbled mess upon hitting the ground and would have been easy targets if the VC had been waiting.

On more than one occasion, we had to clear away jungle growth to make an opening for the incoming choppers to drop our needed supplies of water, ammunition, and food. Much of the time we were at the far ends of field operations, and chopper and artillery support were limited. The 9th was pushing deeper and farther into the surrounding country-side. In many respects we were the vanguard units.

MISSIONS: SEARCH AND DESTROY AND CORDON

The reader may be wondering about the different type of missions we performed. It is important to know that we had had seven grueling (and I mean nose-in-the-dirt) months of intense combat training.

In past wars, soldiers received twelve weeks of training before being shipped off to fight. Our units were not going to be utilizing traditional battle-line tactics but were rather going to engage an elusive and slippery enemy who was comfortable in jungle-type warfare. Oftentimes we'd be beyond the reach of backup artillery or air support, but we were expected to fulfill our many missions no matter how nasty, brutal, or repulsive they may have seemed to civilians back home. This was an in-your-face type of warfare. Our mission was simply to locate, close with, and kill the enemy. We were, like it or not, trained to be a raw, nasty, terrible, and bloody killing machine.

During those many months of hard and intensive training, seven days a week, we had learned many ways to kill. It was as if we had been thrown back to those horrific days of the age of barbarism. It was the lieutenant's duty to hold us in check. We were a pack of wild dogs on search-and-destroy missions, and our leash was the lieutenant's (or sergeant's) mindful commands, which would keep us under control.

Our job in a search-and-destroy mission was to seek out the enemy wherever he was (village, tunnel, base camp, or moving along the Ho Chi Minh Trail) and kill him—no questions asked. Our job was to shoot first, and our training had focused on that simple task of seeking, engaging, and killing the enemy. That was our prime directive. Sorry, we were after raw meat. The country had sent us into battle, and it was either kill or die. Quite simply, combat soldiers had no other option. The jungle-fighting infantryman is trained to do intense battle, nose-to-nose with the enemy.

A lot of people don't truly understand the dynamics that come into play for a combat infantryman, nor do they know how an infantry squad or platoon functions. Contrary to what one might see in war movies, infantrymen do not run around willy-nilly, shooting and killing. In actuality, engagement is generally an orchestrated process of well-practiced and choreographed movements directed toward reaching an objective. As I said earlier, combat is much like football. Losing in combat is not a good option.

A combat infantry squad (or platoon) has two objectives. First, it is to execute the plan of attack and achieve the intended objective. Second, it is to protect the lieutenant. These objectives are achieved with weapons, training, control, discipline, and a superior plan of attack.

When conducting a search-and-destroy mission, we'd follow our attack plan and rely on our experience and training. If we were going to search a village for suspected Viet Cong, we'd approach it and send a couple of squads around to guard the perimeter. The M-60 machine gunner would set up in a strategic location for maximum field-of-fire coverage. The two other squads would approach the village from different directions, and each squad would have its team members positioned and properly spaced. Spacing was important to minimize the possibility of everyone being shot by the enemy. The point man, squad leader, riflemen, grenadier, and explosives guys would each do his thing if we came under attack or discovered a cache of weapons, materials, or ammunition. We all carried an M-16 rifle, but each man had a specialized and highly trained job. It was an individual as well as a team performance.

We had rehearsed this type of mission many times back at Fort Riley, but it was more intense and scary under actual combat conditions. We quickly became adept at moving into a village or suspected camp area and implementing our planned strategy, our combat plan. A night incursion was a more heart-pounding event, but we were just as effective. Sometimes our speed and surprise would yield us not only war materials but also killed or captured VC.

On one such mission—I forget the name of the area—we had been helicoptered into an area with a suspected VC village. We landed about a mile from the village and began traveling down a dusty red dirt road flanked by rice paddies. A slight haze hung in the early morning air, and it was cool and serene. Small hills rose from either side of the valley floor. It was a pretty picture postcard scene.

It had been a 5:00 A.M. landing as five UH-1D troop transport helicopters carrying forty-two battle-hardened combat troops touched down next to a dirt road. As we began walking, we strung ourselves out on either side of the road. We began taking sporadic AK-47 rifle fire from a distant tree line. It wasn't anything heavy, just a few bursts and then the harassers would melt into the foliage. Our grenadiers would fire off a few 20 mm grenades from their M-79 launchers, but that didn't stop the VC. I suspect that they were none too happy about having American GIs tromping through their rice paddies and damaging their young crops.

About the third harassing incident, the lieutenant finally had enough, and he told the second squad, on the right flank, to "Go get those fucking bastards!" (It's not normal for an officer to use profanity among regular troops.) So off goes Sergeant Cruz and his merry band of Cong killers, looking for some action.

Our three other squads approached the village, and Lieutenant Leslie directed me to take Third Squad around the rear of the hooches to block the escape route. As our squad rounded the backside, it happened. Not a dozen feet from my point man out comes a VC with his AK-47. The point man, me, and the VC all surprised each other, but Third Squad was quick on the trigger finger and down went Charlie. "Nice shot, Sarge," said the grenadier who was a few paces behind me.

Instantly we heard gunfire from the front of the village, and it was evident that we had hit upon a VC stronghold. I got Third Squad positioned to block any attempted escape while the other two squads tangled with the front-side action. The brief firefight lasted about five minutes, and the village was secured. We had one guy seriously wounded and three VC dead, including the one tagged by Third Squad, and one captured VC.

Upon hearing the action, Sergeant Cruz and his squad came back from their chase, but they hadn't captured or killed any of our harassers.

We set up for any possible retaliation, and two squads began a systematic search of the village. It was a good find. Ammunition, maps, and equipment were found behind a fake wall. We torched the hooch. Our mission was a success, but that action didn't endear us to the general population of the village. The forthcoming shift in the unification program was still months away. The lieutenant called in a dust-off (medical evacuation by helicopter) for our injured comrade, and he and the captured suspect were airlifted to Bearcat. We spent a big portion of the day searching the surrounding area for camps, tunnels, or other VC locations, and by evening, we were relieved by Bravo Company, which was going to expand the search into the surrounding countryside. We got helicoptered off to another location. Tally-Ho Green!

Bravo Company conducted a search-and-cordon operation that involved encircling the village for a few days and searching each section surrounding the village in a systematic and careful hunt for tunnels, camps, and supply caches.

That was generally how it worked. One unit (platoon or company) would make the initial contact or discovery, and another unit would come in to complete and mop up the area. Our company participated in several search-and-cordon operations, but more often than not, we were the ones who made the initial contact, then we'd move off and let another unit come in to do the mop-up operation. Again, for some reason, we were always on the move, out on point. The tip of the spear. We were either very good at what we did or were being "punished" for some unknown reason. Send in Charlie Company.

I'd like to believe that we ended up being the tip of the spear due to Captain Risor's strong military leadership. He was a true leader with high standards for himself and for his men. He was a career officer, and making a good showing in combat would do much to enhance his career. I'll bet that he would often volunteer his company for the point missions. Whatever the reason, we earned our pay and Combat Infantry Badge. We were darn good at light reconnaissance and ranger-style fighting; it was what we did.

"Men must learn to kill with good conscience if they are to fight successful wars."

—*Will Durant, The Story Of Civilization, Age Of Faith*

OPERATION NIAGARA FALLS

Operations Cedar Falls and Junction City were a couple months away, but we did not know it at the time. What we did quickly realize was that, although scheduled to be a short operation, Niagara would be one of our hottest (combat-wise) and most-intense encounters. It was here that we met our counterpart, the Viet Cong 9th Division, and they were as fierce and mean as the "Old Reliables" of the 9th Infantry Division. This was going to be some head-to-head fighting. Over the next eight months, both divisions were going to be duking it out. It was going to be like a college rivalry.

By this time, we were hard-core, battle-hardened jungle warriors. We had been in half-dozen or so firefights, had suffered a couple of serious casualties, and had kicked some serious butt on old Charlie. However, it was becoming obvious that we were going to be the point unit for the upcoming operations. We were traveling into areas where resupply was limited, air cover sporadic, and artillery support nonexistent. In many pictures, you will see GIs or combat soldiers wearing flak jackets (vests). Flak jackets were worn in case Charlie lobbed in mortar or artillery fire. Where we were going was deep jungle warfare—up close and personal. We would often be just yards if not actually feet away from the enemy, but I don't think that we wore our flak vests after the first couple of weeks of shotgun-dozer duty. As you will see in some of the photos, we did not wear flak jackets. If the extensive amount of gear we carried did not stop shrapnel or bullets, nothing else would either.

We had gone back to Bearcat after a couple weeks in the field, finishing some serious search-and-destroy missions. We spent the first day cleaning our weapons and gear, and, boy did they need it. The rain, muck, and heat were brutal on things. The second day we got mail call, and were we happy! I had the honor of getting the most mail as Mom, Dad, Allen, and family and friends kept me flooded with letters. Mom was the best. She would write every day, without fail, no matter how tired she was. Even the most mundane news—the roses budding or the cat chucking up a hairball—were welcome reminders of home. I would get care packages, lots of them, that would contain a magazine, tooth-

53

paste, or some cookies that I would share with the guys who were not as fortunate. Some guys got little if any mail. I guess they "ain't much for writing in certain parts of the country." What I really craved was a chunk of salami. Some guys wanted cheeseburgers, others catfish, but I wanted salami. When I would get some from Mom, I would selfishly keep it to myself. The mail was now starting to catch up to us. I must have had seventy-five letters and packages to open; some were dated late January/ early February, but it was then mid-April, I think. We had a day to relax, write letters, shower two or three times. While some guys went to the base PX, most of us just lay on our cots and rested.

On day three we were called together and got word that we would be resupplying and moving out. We were given a general idea of the location, but details were vague. The captain told us that we would be trying to make contact with the 9th Viet Cong Division. Either army intelligence did not know the strength of the force or was not going to tell us. But we did discover that we would be loaded for bear with supplies, and pretty much on our own (YOYO = "You're on your own") for the next ten to twelve days. So load us up they did. We packed our rucksacks with ammo, C-rations, plastic explosives, mines, and machine gun ammo. Hey, they even made us carry our own water, one five-gallon container for each squad. (Do you know that five gallons of water weighs thirty-seven pounds?) This was not a good sign. We were going to no man's land. Each man carried between forty and fifty pounds of supplies and gear. We were tired before we boarded the choppers! This time, each squad leader got a map. That was odd. Normally the lieutenant and platoon sergeants had the maps, but not this time. Yep, we would be operating as separate squads, searching out Charlie and the Viet Cong 9th Division. Leave it to the army's Old Reliables. That was us—Cong Killers.

We were getting ready to load onto trucks that would carry us to the helicopters and would soon be on our own for thirteen days without any helicopter or artillery support. Heck, we would not be getting resupplied for five days, but that was only because we burned up almost all of our ammunition in a damn hot firefight.

I do not recall how long the helicopter ride was to the LZ. It seemed like an hour, and it probably was. That was quite an experience even though we had done it dozens of times before. Eight combat-loaded GIs rode along with two door gunners, pilot, and copilot in a UH-1D assault helicopter at 2,500 feet over jungles, rice paddies, rubber plantations, villages, and mangrove swamps—it was a real adventure.

The noise from the motor was droning, and the breeze from the open doors was refreshing. The pilots and door gunners are crazy! They thought that ground-pounding GIs were nuts to fight nose-to-nose, but chopper crews were lunatics. But, that was a good thing when they had to come into a hot area to pick up wounded GIs in a dust-off medical rescue. So, off we went to some far corner of the Vietnamese jungle. We bailed out of the choppers into some yucky swamp that was a foot deep in stagnant water. The choppers did not land; they just hovered while the prop wash kicked up spray and muck, and we were filthy even before we hit the ground (oops, water).

Okay, this was not going to be any picnic. The area we dropped into was all jungle, except for the LZ patch of swamp, half the size of a football field. Our company had gotten the raw end of this deal. Hot! It was 9:30 A.M. and already we were soaked not only from the swamp water but from the 100-degree heat and 112-percent humidity. We moved out smartly, as smartly as one can with fifty pounds of gear weighing you down. We started out as a platoon, but that was not the case for the entire operation.

Right away things got off to a bad start. Leeches! Damn leeches! The area was crawling with bloodsucking leeches! They started latching on to our legs, arms, bodies, and testicles. They were the size of a California slug. Like snails, leeches have 20,000 teeth. They do not hurt when they latch on, but they suck blood. The only way to get them off is to burn them with a match! We could not stop; we had to keep moving, leeches and all. The area was hot, muggy, and bog-like. Our boots sunk into the soggy earth. Walking was hard—our legs ached, but the leeches were getting a free ride. No use taking off the leeches; more would just climb aboard. We have to get to firmer ground.

In these types of operations, movement is not measured in time but in distance. A unit had to be at a certain place, and whether it took three hours or three days, you kept moving until you reached your destination. We tried moving away from the watery terrain, but that seemed to be uphill. The maps were not much help. We were now into a triple-canopy jungle. The vegetation was thick at ground and treetop levels. No sunlight was getting through, thus the ground was wet. We were sweating like mad. The guys on point, hacking away with the machetes had to trade places every five minutes. It was slow going. Those machete guys are good, but it was killer terrain for them. Our progress was slow. The vines were thick, and even guys following behind would be tangled up in the brush.

Now we learned why we had brought along our own water. Although we were used to the heat and humidity, we were sweating profusely. We would have to stop and drink water. We went through our two canteens by noon, so we were glad that we had those five-gallon jugs on our backs. Now it was time to get rid of the leeches as best we could. You do not dare pull them off, as the teeth will stay embedded and the wound will become infected. You can pour insect repellent on them, but why waste mosquito repellent on twenty-plus leeches? As the leech gorges itself on your blood, you strike a match and hold it to the leech until the blood boils and the damn thing explodes and lets go of your skin. I do not know which is worse, the blood-sucking leeches or the ticks and chiggers of the Kansas plains.

I was once telling this story to a fellow at work, and a young female supervisor asked me how we kept our underwear dry in the jungle. I smiled and told her that we went "commando," and she asked what that meant. I told her that we did not wear underwear, and she became all embarrassed. Yep, one had to be very careful when lighting a match to burn off a testicle-sucking leech. You did not want to catch those short hairs on fire!

We pushed on, the sun (if we could have seen it) getting higher and hotter in the sky. We were soaked with sweat. We were not quite sure where we were, as road signs just don't exist in the jungle, and we were too far away from a firebase to request an artillery smoke marking round. We had to rely on our trusty compass headings, tracking counts—141 steps per one hundred yards (thick terrain jungle), and jungle judgment. It is amazing how good of a dead-reckoning land navigator one can become after a few months of jungle travel. We were isolated with no air support and no artillery, if we happened to get into real trouble. Just a map showing massive green with no landmarks. The trouble with those old maps was that they did not indicate the type of terrain, jungle thickness, or even rivers or streams. Just damn green and grid lines. Charlie probably knew where we were; we sure as hell did not have a clue, but we were about to find out.

That night was rough. We were miserable. Hot, wet, tired, and probably lost. Daylight was a relief, although we knew we had to push on.

The next couple of days were not much better, but we were getting use to the routine and terrain. About late afternoon of the third (or fourth) day, we made our first contact. The compass guy (second in line after the machete point) heard noises. We stopped, listened, and confirmed movement to our right flank. It could have been another platoon, but we were not certain. They were probably as lost and as off course as we were. The voices got louder; they were Vietnamese. The jungle vegetation was too thick to do a recon, so we got set for an attack. It sounded like our two forces were on an intersecting course, and then all hell broke loose!

The VC made contact with us; they fired their AK-47s, and we fired our M-16s. It sounded like a battle of popguns until our M-60 machine gunners opened up. Hell, we could not see whom we were shooting at, and they could not see us, but the damn jungle was being cut to shreds. Grenades were not going to work in this tight curtain of vegetation. We just keep firing, reloading, and hoping we would hit them hard enough to hold the line. Smoke was burning off the wet rifle barrels, and guys were starting to run out of ammunition. We would open our rucksacks and get out boxes of ammo, fill our clips, and keep firing. It cost the government one dollar for each bullet fired in combat. We must have greatly increased the national debt that day, because we fired thousands of rounds during those twenty minutes of exchange.

When you are in triple-canopy jungle warfare, you don't pull back, you don't retreat. There is no place to go. The jungle has you in a curtain of vines, brush, and trees that are so thick you cannot see eighteen inches beyond your face. Luck was with us. We were dangerously low on ammo, and some guys had started to fix bayonets. As quickly as it had started, it stopped. The VC pulled away. Gone! Where? We did not quite care; we were just glad that we did not have to try out our hand-to-hand fighting skills.

What a rush! We were not unproven, but even so, the adrenaline was pumping; we were stoked but very low on ammunition. Now we were in a bind. We set up a perimeter—as best we could in the situation—and redistributed what little ammunition we had. The lieutenant called the company commander and apprised him of our situation. We were told to stay in that location and to start clearing an LZ. That was easier said than done. In our jungle setting, just cutting a small trail was a major effort. Trying to cut down vines and trees for a helicopter to land was going to be a serious effort, but we set to work. While some guys worked on the

LZ, others set up a perimeter of Claymore mines and fields of fire. We had no way of knowing if Charlie would attack again. We later learned that we had made contact with the anticipated Viet Cong 9th Division. It was probably a small force, but they had proven to be tough fighters. This would not be the last time we would lock horns with them.

Hours passed, but word finally came that a resupply of ammunition, food, and water was on its way. Hurray! Then we got the call from the chopper that they were inbound our location and for us to "toss smoke." We threw out a couple of yellow smoke grenades, but the chopper could not spot them. We tossed red. No luck. Were we sure of our coordinates? "Hell, no!" The chopper circled. We could hear the rotors but could not see it. Our field of vision was limited to the small opening in the jungle canopy, and that was not very big. Tree limbs obstructed the view. Purple smoke was tossed, and then the chopper pilot radioed that the door gunner had seen smoke a quarter mile away from our stated location and coordinates. Wow, we were really off track. Okay, so the chopper saw our location, but damn, the opening we cut was not large enough for the chopper to land. He had to hover and shove the supplies out the door. They fell to the ground, loads and loads of ammunition, food, but no water. Damn! The water was in plastic containers and would break upon impact. Sorry guys, and off goes the Huey with our precious water. Okay, we needed the ammunition but not so much food. We wanted water, not food. It is amazing how little food one needs after the stomach shrinks to the size of a baby's fist. Even walking through the jungle day after day, we could get by on a couple cans of ham and lima beans or beef stew. Those C-rations are packed with calories.

We loaded up on the ammunition, but what could we do with all that food? We could not leave it; Charlie would find it. So, we used our bayonets to puncture the cans and bury them. This event chewed up most of the day, and then we were behind on our mission. The whole company had to hold position while we regrouped before we started to move again. Over the next few days, other platoons had sporadic contact with the Viet Cong. We had tapped into their supply line, and we were disrupting their movement. We finally got out of the heavy growth and into terrain easier to travel. Squads were sent on frequent recon patrol, looping out two or three hundred meters. Our occasional contact with Charlie was not heavy. It appeared that the Viet Cong, at least at this stage, were not looking for a serious fight. That would come later.

About the tenth day, the four platoons joined up as a company, and for the next three days we moved toward the pickup point. Other companies had had contact with the VC, and the battalion commander proclaimed our operation a success.

NO RAIN IN THE ARMY

It was not always the Viet Cong who caused us fits! If it was not the enemy, then it was the terrain, weather, or the insects. In the jungle we had to contend with triple-canopy foliage and not being able to get our bearings. It was the same thing with the eight-foot-tall elephant grass found in the Iron Triangle. Moreover, we had to contend with the mud of the Delta; if we ever lost a boot from having it sucked right off a foot, we just forgot about finding it—it was gone. Some archaeologist would uncover it 500 years later and wonder about the fellow who lost it.

The heat and humidity was brutal. By midmorning, it might be over 100 degrees and 112 percent humidity. Moreover, when the monsoon rains arrived, they were heavy and stinging. There is an army saying that goes, "It never rains in the army, but it rains on the army." In Vietnam, we encountered so much rain that it became just a routine part of our jungle life. Vietnam sits in the middle of the monsoon region and records rain amounts from 146 inches to 436 inches per year. The coming of rain to the monsoon belt of Southeast Asia is among the most dramatic natural phenomena. One blessed day in June, almost within an hour, the wind may veer 180 degrees, bringing in heavy clouds of moisture. These are the summer monsoon winds.

Monsoon means season, and for six months it blows from the northeast, then it reverses and blows steadily from the southwest.

Forrest Gump, in the movie by the same name, said it best. There is stinging rain, sideways rain, rain that comes up from below, and rain that comes from nowhere.

We were always wet from rain, chest-high stream water, muddy swamps, and rice paddies. We would slosh through muck and be wet for days. Due to the continual dampness, everyone out in the field got jungle rot; trench foot as it was called in World War I and II. Sores would form and not heal due to the moisture. The skin would become so moist it would just peel away and become an infected sore. I was relatively fortunate in that I never got jungle rot too severely, at least not bad enough to pull me out of the field. Some poor guys would have open, bleeding sores for long stretches at a time, and when they become so infected, they had to be shipped to a base camp so they could heal. The best cure was prevention: keeping the feet, legs, and arms dry. I did get heat exhaustion and was sent back to the field hospital for several days. I puked my guts out and could not eat for days.

Sometimes the rains would be welcome, especially if we were hot and dusty or low on water. Most of the time we just lived with the persistent moisture. We would sleep with the rain pelting us, eat soupy C-rations, walk in waterlogged boots, and sometime fight and kill the enemy with wet bullets and muddy rifles. It was an accepted part of our daily life, especially from June through December. It is impossible to stay dry. Water and rain find their way into every dry area of one's being or environment. It is a constant companion of the lowly foot soldier living in the lush jungle, swampy delta, or flooded rice paddies.

LEECHES, SCORPIONS, AND FIRE ANTS

The Viet Cong were usually easy to wrestle with, but the leeches, scorpions, and fire ants had completely different combat tactics. We were never educated about these varmints in basic or even in advanced training. I have already told you about the yucky leeches. Even after a year "in country," we could never figure out how so many of them could become attached to our bodies. You might have a dozen or so all over you, yet they moved slowly, like slugs. They would suck all the blood out of you if you did not burn 'em off. They would gorge themselves and then drop off.

Fire ants were another challenge. Those things were big, no kidding—about three-fourths of an inch long. They would build six- to eight-foot-tall mounds or pull giant tree leaves together and build a nest inside the cavity. Their bite was like a bee sting, only sharper. You have no doubt heard the stories about people being put to death in South Africa by being staked out near a fire ant nest. The things will eat an animal (or human) alive. Soldiers learned early on that it was best to be careful if riding atop an M-60 tank or APC (Armored Personnel Carrier). If a vehicle hit a tree, brushed up against a nest area, or accidentally ran over a mound of ants, those riding on top and inside were in a serious situation. We are talking thousands of mean, nasty, and angry ants swarming for revenge. Everything stops when the ants go on the attack. I felt their stings or a bite on two instances, and it was real torture. Fire ants were probably worse than scorpions. The bite of a fire ant was as intense as being pricked by a rose thorn, and the sting would last for a few seconds. However, multiply that pain by a hundred or so swarming ants landing upon you and constantly biting and you can imagine how your attention is instantly diverted from the mission to battling those painful bites.

When bitten, one would instantly start slapping, hitting, and brushing off the swarming attackers. It might take thirty to sixty minutes to eventually kill enough of them to get things back to normal. The natural defense of fire ants is to bite, so we would have to kill them all or move out of the nest area. And, if the nest had been destroyed, the ants would be swarming over a wide swath. Fortunately, the nests were easy to see, whether a big ball of leaves pulled together and hanging from a tree, or a big mud-mound up to eight feet high. We gave these a wide berth.

On one occasion I was riding atop an APC when the antenna from the preceding carrier brushed against an ant nest, and the ants dropped onto our unit. The other time I was atop a tank when it hit a tree with a nest, knocking thousands of ants on top of us.

Come to think of it, I never had much luck atop tanks or APCs, as you will hear about later.

ON PATROL

Patrol! That is what we did—patrol. We would be helicoptered into an area (jungle, rice paddies, elephant grass, mangrove swamp, laterite[4] fields, or near a suspected Viet Cong village) and then would set about search-and-destroy missions. We attempted to make contact with the Viet Cong, discover tunnel complexes, or push him in a direction to disrupt his supply lines. Patrols could go for days without contact. We would walk for long distances, slugging it out against hostile terrain, and then suddenly we would be in a firefight, burning up twenty rounds of ammo every five seconds. Firefights might last just a few minutes or might turn into hide-and-seek encounters that could last for several hours.

Our units (platoons, companies, and battalions) always seemed to be on the forward edge of the fighting, and we were always poking and prodding the VC. Most of these contacts were platoon- or squad-size encounters. They were generally against the Viet Cong and not the highly trained North Vietnamese regulars, who were found further north in I Corp. My recall is that I was in well over two dozen firefights during my tour of duty (that's what it was called...one year). The number could have been many more. Jim Haines from Bravo Company reminded me of several firefights that I had completely forgotten. Most of them were against small incursions of five to twenty VC. I can recall one major encounter where the enemy size seemed larger than a platoon (over forty), but that was a hot LZ and we were on a company mission. These small firefights were usually brief—five to ten minutes—but very intense. Lots of heavy firing on both sides, and then the VC would melt away, usually taking their dead and wounded. Poof—they'd be gone.

Water and ammo were always a concern. Fresh water was always welcome, but we seldom got it. We would fill up our canteens whenever possible, which was usually some stagnant stream. We would drop iodine tablets into the canteen to kill the germs. After a couple of months, we did not even notice the foul taste. We had been issued one canteen

4 Laterite is a red, residual soil containing large amounts of aluminum and ferric hydroxides formed by the decomposition of many kinds of rocks and found especially in well-drained tropical rain forests. It gets into your skin and you end up looking like a Red Man.

with our gear, but over time, we learned to beg, borrow, or steal a second or third one. On one patrol, we were running low on water when we came across a slow-running stream. We stopped and set up a fast perimeter so we could take turns getting a quick "bath" and refill our canteens. We then moved out, heading upstream. About 200 yards farther, we came across a decaying Vietnamese body lying in the water. No one emptied their canteen; water was too precious.

Once a month the medic would come along and give each man a quinine pill to prevent malaria. Those were horse pills, but they worked. I cannot recall anyone ever getting sick. Injuries, yes; sick, not really. It must have been all those shots back in AIT.

AGENT ORANGE

One of the militarily effective but environmentally damaging methods of uncovering the Viet Cong's strongholds was through the use of the defoliant known as Agent Orange. This chemical would be sprayed from C-130 aircraft over a large jungle area, usually a triple canopy, and the result would be a barren landscape stripped of it leaves and foliage. Air reconnaissance would photograph the terrain for suspected tunnel or stronghold complexes, and the infantry would be sent in to investigate, locate, and eradicate any Viet Cong. The chemical was fast acting, and usually within a few days, the once lush jungle would be nothing but a sea of leafless trunks and branches with the once bog-like jungle floor being exposed to the tropical sun for the first time in eons.

I can recall a couple of search-and destroy-missions in a defoliated area, and once we even trampled through a thick jungle area that was still dripping from what I suspect was a defoliant. Overall, our unit didn't have much contact with AO; encountering it maybe half a dozen times. We were at the "tip of the spear," so to speak. Sniff and spook missions; Light reconnaissance and ranger style tactics, in trying to locate the VC. After we found their strongholds, we would report it and move on, then those areas would be sprayed with A.O. and other units would come in to eradicate them. We were oftentimes well beyond the boundaries of meaningful support.

To date I have had no affects from my limited exposure to Agent Orange, but a young lieutenant who was a family friend and close friend to my brother, Allen, did die from cancer directly related to Agent Orange.

The many small, non-lethal skin cancers removed from my hands and arms probably were caused by exposure to the tropical sun.

SNAKES (OR THE BOA CONSTRICTOR STORY)

Well, we had fire ants, scorpions, leeches, and, of course, snakes. The flying snakes were actually that; they sailed through the air from tree to tree. Others included small (eight to twelve inches long), deadly tree snakes, but our favorite (if you can call it that) was the boa constrictor. We had been on patrol in some easy terrain—light jungle. It was a more-relaxed patrol, but we had not had any contact for several days, and some of the guys were getting itchy fingers. They wanted to tangle it up with Charlie. This time we were in a restricted-fire zone.

Of the two types of zones, the "free-fire zone" was one in which you could fire your weapon for any reason, without permission. You could shoot at animals, clear your weapon, or take target practice. We would test fire our weapons at least once a day to ensure that the rounds were not getting jammed in the chamber due to heat, moisture, or dirt. In a restricted-fire zone, however, you could not fire your weapon unless directly fired upon or without permission from the sergeant or lieutenant. In restricted fire zones there were usually other units working in proximity, so you did not want any "friendly-fire" accidents. It is generally not a good idea to keep a round "locked and loaded" in the chamber for that very reason—jamming. But if Charlie was going to take a pop shot at you (as he often did), you did not want to waste those extra seconds loading a round into the chamber while Charlie is firing away at your young ass. Thank you, Lemar Jackson. Contrary to conventional wisdom, everyone kept a round in the chamber. It often meant the difference between life and death.

We had been moving as a company; the four platoons moved in four columns about a hundred meters apart. We had stopped for a rest break when the lieutenant told me to take my squad out for a recon (reconnaissance) patrol. That is when we would patrol in a small loop, maybe go out fifty or a hundred yards and circle back, checking to see that no enemy was in that area. In this case, it was a lightly vegetated area. At about the apex of the loop, all of a sudden Fitzwater—"the squad scamp" —fired three shots from his M-16!

"What in the hell are you doing, Fitzwater?" I yelled.

"Snake, Sarge!" he replies. Yep. The three rounds he had pumped into a twelve-foot-long boa constrictor that had been stretched out against a log generally ended the snake's afternoon nap. When our radioman whacked off the snake's head with a machete, its powerful jaws snapped open. He took the detached head and shoved it into the plastic radio battery bag.

"What in the fuck are you going to do with that?" I asked.

"I'm going to take it back as a trophy, Sarge."

"You guys are crazy," I told them.

Then one of the guys piped up: "You know, Sarge, they always travel in pairs."

"Okay you clowns, let's get the fuck out of here and finish up the recon."

"Tally-Ho Green!"

What a crazy bunch—God's Lunatics! Combat does strange things to people; it really does. It is a completely different mindset and psyche. It is a no-holds-barred situation, and the survival mode runs high, especially for combat troops deeply entrenched in the trials and tribulations of "in-your-face" combat conditions. It is either kill or be killed! After your first enemy contact, you simply are not afraid of anything or anyone. It is like being thrust into a no-lose arena, and you will do anything to gain the upper hand. You are in the constant fight mode. Every part of your body is on alert to fight, attack, and kill if necessary. That is why guys will charge into an enemy stronghold, into the face of deadly fire, without a moment's thought. They will run out into a blizzard of bullets to rescue a fallen buddy and think nothing of it. Fear, danger, and death's consequences do not enter your mind.

There is a place in the back of the mind that is a black void. It resides in dark crevices that never see the light of reason. No one can explain it, and outsiders will never understand it. Combat infantrymen are a stand-alone breed. They have been to the other side and, if lucky, have returned. Most of us did not like returning to base camp at Bearcat. After a couple of days of relaxation we would start to lose our fighting edge, and that was dangerous. Our entire bodies were trained to fight, kill, and destroy. Too much rest was our "enemy." We looked death in the face every day.

"It would be absurd to expect soldiers to be saints. Good killing requires its own unique virtues."

—*Will Durant, The Story Of Civilization, Age Of Faith*

OPERATION CEDAR FALLS

Operation Cedar Falls was the warm-up to the upcoming Junction City operation. For us in the 39th Infantry Brigade, 9th Infantry Division, the two operations ran together as one. We started out by moving into the Iron Triangle[5], an area north of Saigon. The Viet Cong had held this region since the early 1950s, when the French were fighting them. Now it was time for the 9th Infantry Division to move in and roust them out.

Our boundaries were to be the area between highways 1 and 13. We had tangled with the Viet Cong on many occasions, and we got lots of help from the big guns, including 105s and self-propelled 155s. So, we went into this hotbed of enemy territory. Charlie was not too happy at having his secure little area disturbed. The job of the 9th and the 25th divisions was to make his life miserable, and that we did. When Charlie got mad, he tried to get even. We would punch at him, and he would poke at us.

I need to tell the trip-flare story. When a platoon or squad sets up in a nighttime defensive position, they usually will put out a series of trip flares and/or Claymore mines. The flares are usually several meters out in front of the string of mines so that if the enemy does try to infiltrate, he will more than likely trip off a flare and illuminate the area. This helps to identify the target—Charlie. Claymore mines are about the size of a sheet of paper, seven by ten inches, and about two inches thick and filled with C-4, a plastic (think Play-Doh) explosive that is impregnated with sharp metal fragments. An electric blasting cap that is triggered by a squeeze handle activates the mine. These mines are wicked.

---

5 The Iron Triangle was a sixty-square-mile (155-square kilometer) area in the Binh Duong province of Vietnam, so named due to its being a stronghold of Viet Minh activity during the war. The region had been under control of the Viet Minh throughout the French war in Vietnam and continued to be so throughout the American war, despite concerted efforts on the part of U.S. and South Vietnamese forces to destabilize the region as a power base for their enemy. The Iron Triangle was between the Saigon River on the west and the Tinh River on the east, and it bordered Route 13, about twenty-five miles (40 kilometers) north of Saigon. The southern apex of the "triangle" was seven miles (11 kilometers) from Phu Cong, the capital of Binh Duong Province. Its proximity to Saigon was both a reason for American and South Vietnamese efforts to eradicate it as well as why it remained a crucial area for Communist forces to maintain control over.   —Wik*ipedia.*

My buddy and I had dug our foxhole for the night and set out our trip flares and Claymores. When I went out in the morning to take them down, I discovered that one of the mines had been turned around, facing our position. Now one might say that we had set it up wrong, but the live hand grenade used to trigger the booby trap had been removed. Yikes, Charlie had come up during the night and done his deed, but something had spooked him. Had he finished his sabotage, he would have provoked us into firing off the Claymore, thus killing or maiming ourselves. That incident had a profound effect on me. Somehow, someway, we had dodged a major bullet.

Another time, as we moved out for patrol, I tripped a wire and set off a trip flare. It had been one set by another platoon, but they had missed removing it. It scared the be-jibbers out of me, and the lieutenant was pissed. He lectured me on being more alert and chewed out the lieutenant of the offending platoon. A good lesson for all concerned. Had it been booby-trapped with a hand grenade rather than a trip flare, I would not be writing this.

Jungle warfare is tough in many ways, not the least of which is the amount of supplies and ammunition that has to be carried for a self-contained unit such as an infantry squad or platoon. C-4 is an explosive compound used in mines, as we had learned, but it also comes in a brick form for blowing tunnels, trees, and large objects. Nobody liked carrying extra mortar rounds, M-60 machine gun ammo, or other supplies, but no one ever complained about carrying extra bricks of good old C-4. You see, C-4, though activated by an electrical charge, can also burn as a little blue flame when pinched off the brick and lit with a match. It is a wonderful compound to be used to heat cold C-rations. Just light a little C-4 and hold the can (using the lid as a handle) over the blue flame, and you can have hot beef stew, ham and lima beans, or cocoa. Of course, the officers always reminded us not to use the C-4 for warming our food—it was for combat use only. Not only did we ignore the order, but also the officers themselves used C-4 to prepare a hot meal. Ah, the pretty blue flames all throughout the camp. Nice. (Right, Lieutenant Joseph Zukin, Jr.?)

THE QUEEN'S ARMY

One mission during Operation Don Ched involved patrolling an area thick with vegetation in a no-fire zone. We were doing a company sweep, and the four platoons were moving in a column formation, spaced a hundred meters apart. The particular area for first platoon happened to be on uneven terrain of small rises and gullies.

As we were moving along, the lead squad signaled the platoon to halt, and as we were beginning to crouch down, a hail of bullets came at us out of the jungle. Hell, we started returning fire with all we had. The machine gunner started blasting away with his M-60 machine gun, and the jungle was being cut to shreds. We were burning through the ammunition, but we had no clue as to what or who we were shooting at. We assumed that we were the targets of a Viet Cong ambush but had no visual confirmation.

The lieutenant radioed the company commander, who confirmed that no other platoons in the company were firing, so we knew it was not our own people. The lieutenant received permission to call in artillery rounds. As the lieutenant gave our coordinates to the firebase for the initial marking round to confirm our location, the firebase also received a similar request from a different unit at nearly the same coordinates.

Some sharp officer sitting in the fire control center quickly put two and two together and realized that first platoon of Charlie Company and a unit from our allies of the Royal Thai Army's Queen Volunteer Regiment both wanted to fire on each other! Yikes! Both sides were ordered to cease firing!

A patrol from each side was sent out and made contact. We discovered that the Thai troops were in a gully in the wrong area and fired on us, thinking we were VC. The Thai government had sent 2,000 men to fight in Vietnam, and the unit was attached to the 9th Infantry Division.

It was reported that neither side sustained any injuries during that hot and intense firefight. What does that say about either side's marksmanship? A good example of good and bad communication.

BETTER NOT FLUNK MAP READING

In advanced individual training, map reading was a big part of our curriculum. Lieutenants and sergeants were expected to be well versed in this combat skill. Our lives depended upon it, as proved the case in our battle with the Thai Army.

Those guys firing the 88 and 105 howitzers can put a shell into a square no larger than ten feet by ten feet, the size of a bedroom in a bungalow. And, they can do it from five miles away.

Maps are laid out in grid squares of 1,000 feet. These squares are further subdivided into markings of 100 feet and 10 feet. When calling in a location or requesting fire support (artillery or air power), the coordinates are given in a series of six numbers, three for the X-axis and three for the Y-axis. The intersecting point is the intended location. If that is where a unit is requesting a shell or bomb, you can be darn certain that that is where it will land.

Usually, a unit would request a "marking" round of smoke to be fired and explode at a location a couple hundred feet from the intended location. This permitted coordinate adjustments to be made before the "hot" round hit its mark.

Thank goodness that our lieutenant and the Thai officer were accurate in their mapping coordinates and that someone in fire control realized that two friendly forces wanted to fire upon each other.

THE INFAMOUS
BANANA LEAF STORY

This is one of my brother's (Allen) and nephew's (Tod) favorite stories, one that shook me to the core. It is funny now, but it scared the living daylights out of me one night.

We had been on a hard patrol through the jungle, and we were all pretty bushed. Much of the day's travel had been through triple-canopy vegetation and thick underbrush. We had traveled well into darkness before stopping and had settled down in a "free-fire zone," one in which anyone can fire a weapon for any reason—to clear it or to shoot at animals, VC, or whatever. Corporal Farmer and I had a spot together, and he agreed to take the first watch, which was fine with me. I was bushed. Farmer woke me up after a couple of hours. As he was lying down on his poncho, I looked up and noticed what I thought was a crouched-down Viet Cong wearing a soft cap. I intently watched him for movement, but he was still. I thought about tossing a grenade, but he was too close—about fifteen feet away. If I fired my M-16, the muzzle flash would have given away our position. What to do? I decided the best thing was to fire my M-16. I poked Farmer and told him I saw a VC in front of our position and asked him to cover me. He rolled over and looked out at the area I had identified and reported, "There's nothing there!" I swore to him I could see the VC. He told me I was crazy, but he agreed to cover me, so I pumped three quick rounds into the "VC." Nothing moved. I watched for a long time. Farmer again told me that I had been seeing things and that the moonlight was just casting shadows. With that, he rolled over and was fast asleep. I watched that object all night, tired as I was. I knew it was a VC!

At dawn, Farmer awoke and asked why I had not had him take another watch. I then cautiously went out to check the object and discovered in the early morning light that I had pumped three perfectly aimed rounds into a big banana plant leaf. Well, at least I had grouped my shots; my old rifle instructor would have been proud. It took me a *long* time to live that one down. "Hey, Weitzel! You seen any banana leaves today?"

74

HUNKER DOWN

While on jungle patrol, we would stop at a spot for the night and set up a defensive circular perimeter. If we had traveled long and hard and it was late, we would just "circle the wagons" and lay out our ponchos with two men per location. That was not the best method, but sometimes that's all that time would allow. If we stopped earlier, then we would take out our trenching tool (a small shovel) and scrape away some dirt, creating a shallow spot to lie in. We would use the dirt we shoveled out to build a protective mound around our foxhole.

The ideal situation would be to dig a foxhole three or four feet deep and build a protective mound of dirt around it to protect from bullets and mortar and artillery shelling. Then we would clear away the brush in front of our foxhole and create a fan-shaped field of fire, a clearing that would go out about thirty to fifty feet. About forty feet out we would place two or three trip flares. These were beer-can-size canisters that were partially buried and connected to each other by a small trip wire. The wire would be looped through the loosened safety pin. If something or someone hit the trip wire, the pin would be pulled out of the flare and everything would be suddenly illuminated with a white light.

Fifteen feet back from the trip flares we would place two or three Claymore mines in a fan-shaped pattern. The men in the foxholes could electrically detonate the mines, an effective defense when the VC tried to attack and accidentally tripped the flare wires. A backup mine might be positioned ten feet behind the two forward mines.

The flares, mines, and field of fire would afford a good defensive position. Watching our particular zone from our foxhole, we would have several hand grenades lying close by, should we need them.

Of course, all of this depended on each soldier staying alert, watching its area, and not falling asleep. Every combat infantryman will freely admit to having fallen asleep at his post more than once.

We would often booby-trap our mines with hand grenades. This was a tricky and dangerous but necessary procedure. We would set the Claymore mine over a partially buried hand grenade and then remove the safety pin. Replacing the pin the next morning required careful skill

75

and attention. Surprisingly, it became so routine that we seldom thought much about it until someone made a fatal mistake. Then we became conscious of our actions.

Quite often, we would have an animal or a VC trigger a trip flare or mess with a Claymore mine and BOOM—the whole place would light up! We would blast away with our M-16s and toss grenades. Better to be safe than sorry.

After setting up in a night defensive position, we never went out in front of the position to take a nighttime potty break. No—not a good idea.

OPERATION JUNCTION CITY

O f course, those of us slugging it out in the jungle and rice paddies did not know it at the time, but we were about to become the major element in a major operation of the war. Operation Junction City—and its counterpart, Cedar Falls—would pit the U.S. 9th Infantry against the Viet Cong 9th Infantry in the major turning point of the war. For the operation's seventy-seven days we faced our foe in his backyard and put another Presidential Unit Citation on our proud ribbon.

It has been said that the Cedar Falls and Junction City operations were turning points in the Vietnam War. I do not know about that, but it certainly proved that the 9th Infantry Division was one crack unit and that individually we had learned the rules of the jungle. We slugged it out with the Viet Cong 9th Division in some nasty firefights, heated battles, and nighttime attacks, but the final tally was overwhelmingly in favor of the U.S. Army and the 9th Division.

Mom and Dad wrote that they had seen television news clips about the Junction City Operation. While the artillery, tanks, and Hueys were attacking from one direction, the infantry was slugging it out against Charlie in the marshy swamps, jungle, and elephant grass on the ground. On one deep patrol into the heart of the Iron Triangle, our platoon stumbled upon a major tunnel complex. It happened by chance, as the platoon was patrolling in a suspected stronghold area. Before I explain our contribution to the patrol, let me tell the story of Lemar Jackson and how he saved my life.

We were pushing deep into VC territory through thick terrain. It was hot, and we were on the move. Third Squad had just rotated from the point position, hacking through the vegetation, to the "rest" position in the rear. I was second from the end, and Lemar, a big black man from Mississippi, was the last. The lieutenant was up front with First Squad, and the whole platoon was strung out pretty far. We were moving along, trying to keep pace with the group. Lemar was about ten paces behind me, acting as rearguard. I heard a sharp snap behind me, and thinking that Lemar had stepped on a jungle vine, I turn to look, and my world went into slow motion. Lemar had turned to his rear, and about twenty feet behind on the trail we had just trampled was a VC in black pajamas. Lemar's bullets were just hitting the VC in the stomach and chest as the VC first bent forward and then recoiled. He had fired at us with his AK-47, missing us both. Lemar had been quick for a big fella. As the Cong fell, Lemar turned back to me—everything still in slow motion—and said, "I got 'em, Sarge!"

"Goooooooooood," was my reply.

That VC had been out to bag a couple of GIs, but Lemar had luckily been on his toes. The column did not stop. By the time we caught up with them, they were some twenty-five meters ahead. I worked my way up to the front to tell the lieutenant, but by the time I reached him, we were at least a half-mile from the ambush site.

It was later that afternoon that we stumbled upon the tunnel complex, and it turned out to be a major stronghold. We had smelled food cooking and entered a small clearing with an open fire and pots of boiling rice. Charlie was gone, but we found his tunnel entrance, and the platoon's two "tunnel rats" (TRs) set to work exploring the complex. The lieutenant had us set up a perimeter, and the TRs set off a few Claymore mines to clear the entrance areas. As they worked their way through the tunnels, they found caches of rice, ammunition, maps, and weapons. Charlie had made a hasty retreat. Exit holes were found some 200 meters away, and the complex was large. The lieutenant called the company commander, who arrived about an hour later. Then the battalion commander showed up. The rice, supplies, and weapons were gathered and stacked, and a couple of helicopters were flown in and loaded with the booty.

We did not stay around, but we heard an intelligence detail came, mapped the tunnel complex, and then blew it up. Then we were back on patrol—keeping Charlie on the move and off-balance. The operation ground on for us. It had been just another day.

"In war, people go to extraordinary extremes," – Plato

Top: Summer, 1966, recruit Warren P. Weitzel, Fort Riley, Kansas. (Photo: Author's collection) **Bottom:** A cheerful Warren P. Weitzel, having completed basic training, prepares for a two-week leave to California. Company mess hall in the background. 1966, Fort Riley, Kansas; Camp Forsyth. (Photo: Author's collection)

Example of recruits in training; bayonet training. (Photo: 9th Infantry Yearbook)

Pugil stick training. Not Weitzel's favorite exercise. (Photo: 9th Infantry Yearbook)

Soldier holding an M-16 automatic weapon. (Photo: 9th Infantry Yearbook)

Top: Two weeks into AIT training, Fall, 1966. 3rd Squad, 1st Platoon, "Charlie" Company, 4th Battalion, 39th Infantry, 9th Infantry Division, Fort Riley Kansas. Private Fitzwater, fourth from left, back row. Private James Farmer, last on right, back row, Sergeant Warren Weitzel, front row, right. All part of God's Lunatics. (Photo: 9th Infantry Yearbook) **Bottom:** The 9th Division readiness made national news. (Newspaper clipping: Author's collection)

Probably To Mekong

9th Heading Out Soon

(Special to The Mercury)
FORT RILEY — Informed sources said here today the first mass movements of the 9th Infantry Division to Viet Nam will start Sunday morning rather than tonight as had been reported earlier.

The start of airlifting troops of the 3rd Brigade of 9th Division to West Coast ports of embarkation is slated to start from the Manhattan Municipal Airport Sunday morning and will continue at intervals until the entire brigade is moved in about two weeks.

The 1st Brigade is expected to move out in December and the 2nd in January.

Whether a new division will replace the 9th at Fort Riley is still a subject of speculation, although some reliable source indicated the post will not get a new division, but will concentrate on training.

Although Fort authorities would neither confirm or deny the movement of the 9th Division to Viet Nam — in keeping with military policy — it has been known for some time that Maj. Gen. George S. Eckhardt, division commander, left the post earlier this week. Brig. Gen. John A. Seitz is now acting as division as well as post commander.

Another rumor that has been circulating for some time now that the 9th Division was going into the Mekong Delta area appeared to be fairly - well confirmed today. Reports are that the division's heavy equipment has been directed to that area. If, as it appears, the 9th goes to the delta area it would be in keeping with recent reports that the United States intends building up its forces in that

hot-bed of Viet Cong. U. S. authorities are known to feel that the delta is the most urgent area both for military offensives as well as civilian pacification programs.

The 9th already has an advance party of about 800 men in Viet Nam. They have been there since September, reportedly.

The 3rd Brigade of the 9th should be in Viet Nam within about a month. It takes about 21 days by boat from the West Coast.

It is expected that the 9th Division will be joining a combined command of U. S. and Vietnamese troops in the II Field Force, commanded by Lt. Gen. Jonathan O. Seaman, a former commanding general of the 1st Infantry Division in Viet Nam and at Fort Riley.

Paul, Bea, and Warren Weitzel, October, 1966, in the front yard of their Santa Clara, California home. On leave from Fort Riley, Kansas, before being shipped overseas. (Photo: Author's collection)

November 1966. Soldiers on the troop train to Oakland, California. We carried our weapons everywhere during our nineteen months of training and combat. (Photo: Jim Haines collection)

82

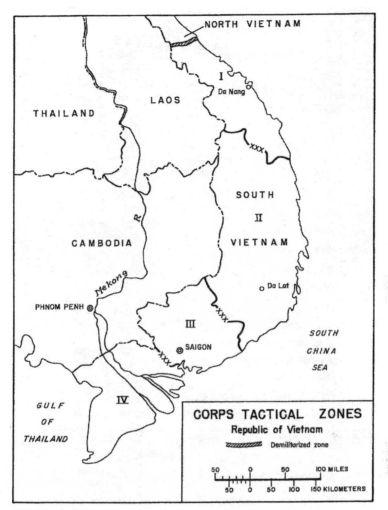

Corps Tactical Zones map. The 9th Division fought in III & IV Corp, War Zone C. That's where the V.C. was most intensely concentrated. (Photo: Department of The Army, Vietnam Studies, Cedar Falls and Junction City)

Top: Sergeant Warren Weitzel "in country," enjoying his new scenery and surroundings. (Photo: Author's collection) **Bottom:** Private James Farmer sitting atop a bunker at Du Puy. (Photo: Author's collection)

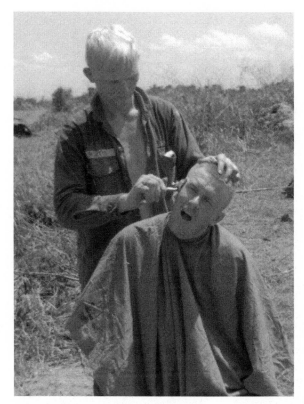

Top: Spec 4, Jim Haines, Bravo Company, (right) getting a GI haircut in the field, from the skilled hands of Private Ray Martin. Who needs Supercuts! (Photo: Jim Haines collection) **Bottom Left:** Sergeant Warren Weitzel digging a foxhole for a night defensive position. Iron Triangle, April 1967. (Photo: Author's collection) **Bottom Right:** Spec 4, Jim Haines, Bravo Company, setting up his foxhole with his M-16 and M-72 LAW, Light Anti-Tank Weapon. (Photo: Jim Haines collection)

Left: Sergeant Warren Weitzel unhappy because he's out of C-4 explosive, and he's ready to heat up his C-rations. (Photo: Author's collection) **Right:** Sergeant Warren Weitzel in the jungle. Vietnam, 1967. Operation Junction City, Iron Triangle. Search and destroy mission. Photo taken by combat photographer assigned to Warren's platoon during the mission. (Photo: Author's collection)

Huey cruising along at 2,500 feet. (Photo: Jim Haines collection)

Top: Soldier on patrol in typical Vietnam jungle conditions. (Photo: US Army, 9th Infantry Division, Vietnam, Combat Art and Photography Book, 1966 -1967, APO San Francisco, 96370, Commanding General, MG G. G. O'Connor) **Bottom:** Door gunner manning an M-60 machine gun on a UH-1D Huey helicopter. (Photo: 9th Infantry Yearbook)

Top Left: Vietnamese POW, captured by Bravo Company, north of Bien Hoa. (Photo: Captain George Skinner, Bravo Company collection, courtesy of Jim Haines) **Top Right:** Vietnamese children. (Photo: Author's collection) **Bottom:** Perimeter bunker positions at an artillery base camp, looking toward the Black Virgin Mountain. (Photo: Author's collection)

Top: "Sorry, Sir, I buried my 50-ton tank up to its ass in mud!" Junction City II operation near the Black Virgin Mountain area. (Photo: Author's collection) **Bottom:** A sample of a C-Ration Letter written by Warren, February 1967. (Photo: Author's collection.)

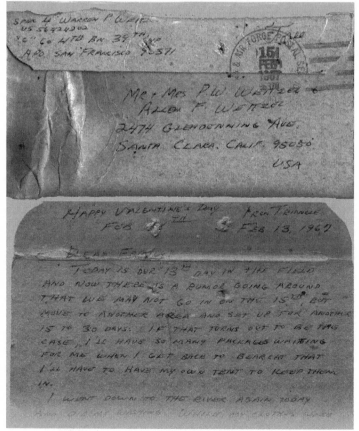

Rifle squad riding atop an M-48 tank. (Photo: Jim Haines collection)

Combat troops aboard a brown water launch on a riverine mission in the Delta Region. (Photo: Jim Haines collection)

Troops boarding C-130 Cargo Planes. Heading north for Xuan Loc to assist the 25th Division. (Photo: Jim Haines collection)

90

Top Left: The Octofoil is the 9th Infantry Division emblem. Scanned from Warren Weitzel's actual Octofoil patch. (Author's collection) **Top Right:** Army Commendation Metal (Example taken from the Internet) **Bottom:** Warren P. Weitzel's Certificate Of Combat Service. (Author's Collection)

CERTIFICATE

OF

COMBAT SERVICE

C COMPANY, 4TH BATTALION, 39TH INFANTRY

BE IT KNOWN TO ALL MEN THAT

WARREN P WEITZEL _____ SERVED WITH THE 9TH INFANTRY DIVISION IN ARMED CONFLICT AGAINST INSURGENT FORCES IN THE REPUBLIC OF VIETNAM.

Vietnam War 1964 – 1975 service certificate. (Author's Collection)

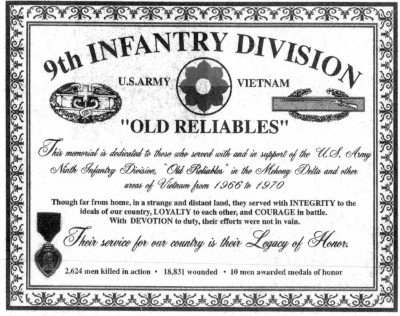

9th Infantry Division Certificate for service in Mekong Delta Region, 1966-1970. (Author's Collection)

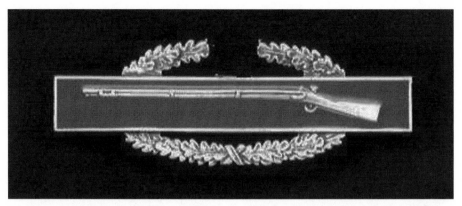

The Combat Infantryman Badge (CIB) is the U.S. Army combat service recognition decoration awarded to soldiers—enlisted men and officers (commissioned and warrant) holding Colonel rank or below, who personally fought in active ground combat while an assigned member of either an infantry or special forces unit of brigade size or smaller, any time after 6 December 1941. (Wikipedia)

March/April, 1967. Sergeant Warren Weitzel, preparing to leave base camp to begin Operation Niagara Falls. The water carrier on Weitzel's back weighs 37 pounds, alone. (Author's Collection)

Top Left: Paul, Bea, and Allen Weitzel, 1966 or early 1967, at their Santa Clara, California home. Allen wearing his Frontier Village Amusement Park ride operator uniform. Standing in front of the family's red Cadillac that was used on the drive to Oklahoma to pick up Warren when he was discharged. (Photo: Author's collection) **Top Right:** January, 1968. Bea, Warren, and Paul Weitzel in the back yard of their Santa Clara, California home. Warren was on leave, after his tour of duty in Vietnam, before being assigned to Fort Sill, Oklahoma. Warren is pictured with some, but not all of his military ribbons and awards. (Photo: Author's collection)

January, 1968. Close up of Sergeant Warren Weitzel, displaying some of his military ribbons, medals, and awards. (Photo: Author's collection)

Joseph Zukin, Jr., Warren's mentor, 2011. (Photo: Joseph Zukin, Jr. collection)

Allen F. Weitzel, Warren's younger brother. Contact: www. witent.com (Photo: Susan Weitzel collection)

VISUAL IMPRINTS

Every GI has indelible visual imprints. I can see the thick jungle, mucky mangrove swamps, and the stark, grey, landscape where Agent Orange had been sprayed and had killed all vegetation. Then there were the huge bomb craters with pools of stagnant water in the bottoms and whitish-grey earth for a hundred meters in all directions. From January 1966 to October 1966, B-52 bombers dropped 600,000 tons of bombs. During those bombing runs, the sound must have been deafening.

The Viet Cong liked to travel and attack at night. I guess they felt the darkness gave them greater cover, and it probably did. GIs did not like to fight or travel at night; Charlie had the advantage there. We would call in Huey support due to attacks on our night perimeter. I do not recall any big incursions, but even the small, harassing ones were scary enough for me. Boy, those gunships were wicked. They had rocket launchers, Gatling guns, and M-60 machine guns mounted on either side. A few passes around the perimeter by those bad boys and Charlie got the message pretty darn fast. Those red tracer rounds gave a good indication of where the action was being concentrated. We would light our perimeter boundaries with starburst flares. "Thanks, guys—We appreciate the air support."

Much of the time we were fortunate in having access to Huey air support, but there were times when we were beyond the range of any meaningful artillery support. We could get air support, but marking our exact location was not always easy in a triple-canopy environment, so we did not want to have those gunships firing on us. We would prefer to take care of matters ourselves if we could. On more than one occasion, we ended up being off course and too close to friendly fire from our own choppers or artillery. This happened to me one time when I took the squad for an extended (700- meter) recon patrol and ran off the map and into another section where the mortar platoon was test firing. A good radioman got them to cease fire, and when we came through their perimeter, we got some nasty comments, and rightfully so. We (I) had messed up. Jungle travel was not an exact science; we didn't have GPS back then.

SGT. WEITZEL'S BIG TEST

As Operation Junction City wound down, we moved south into the Mekong Delta to help the Riverine units, which used brown water-craft rather than helicopters as a means of travel. Riverine units traveled in shallow-draft boats up and down the many rivers and streams in the delta, and troops disembarked and waded through the marshy country-side, trying to make contact with Charlie. The 9th Division had three separate bases in Vietnam: Dong Tam, Tan An, and the main base at Camp Bearcat. The Dong Tam base was a Riverine unit in the South Delta region.

About midtour, I was ordered to report for duty to the southern Riverine unit, but for some unknown reason my orders were cancelled, and I stayed with the 4th Battalion. That was fine with me. It was nearing the end of June 1967, and we had been "in country" for six months. We had just gotten a new platoon lieutenant, Lieutenant Walker, who was just out of West Point. I remember the day he arrived at our unit in freshly starched fatigues, clean as a whistle. Here we were, bloodied, muddied, and deeply tanned from the tropical sun; he was fair-skinned. Lieutenant Walker was a nice guy, about my age, twenty-three, but green. He was textbook smart—very—and I was an experienced, battle-hardened jungle warrior. We bonded. He was very respectful of our experience, even when it went contrary to his leadership training. Among the first things one of the guys told the young lieutenant was that he should lose the pretty gold lieutenant bars on his helmet and collar. Charlie would have loved to have targeted in on those in his gun sights. The lieutenant quickly complied. Lieutenant Walker listened to his men, respected their wisdom, and set about learning how a real war was fought.

A few days after he joined us, I was called to the CP (command post). We had just set up a night perimeter with Claymore mines, trip flares, and fields of fire. A call to the CP usually meant either a recon patrol or night ambush; I was hoping for the former. The lieutenant told me he had a mission for me. *"We need to secure a landing zone for a new artillery base to be established some 9,000 meters (five miles) from this location. The spearhead contingent will be helicoptered in at 0530*

hours, followed at 0600 by an airlift of 88s and 105s. You are to take
your squad, avoid all contact, and reach the LZ by 0500 and secure it.
There will be no available artillery cover. You will have a radioman so
you can communicate with the incoming choppers, but there is to be no
other radio contact. Get your guys ready. We'll alert the line that there
is an outbound unit, and you will leave through Delta sector. Second
and First squads will take over your vacated positions. Any questions?"

"No, sir!"

"Okay. Here's a map and the LZ location. This is a critical mission. Good luck. Now move 'em out."

Nine thousand meters is a long walk, even in daylight hours. On flat, level terrain with fully loaded gear, it would be a push, but doing a night patrol through rice paddies, staying off roads, and avoiding villages as well as the VC was going to be a challenge. Everyone was tired. I went back to the squad and told them the news; it was not well received, but they quickly fell into line. I checked the map and looked for the best route. With gear secure, radio ready, and map in hand, we started out through the cleared field-of-fire opening in the perimeter. Many other squads were looking at us, and they were glad that they had not received the assignment. The distance on the map did not look far, but believe me, this assignment was no walk in the park. As we moved through the lines, I wondered what challenges we would face for the next seven hours. This was a big challenge for me. I had taken the guys on night recons—500 to 700 meters out—and set up night ambushes, but never this distance without serious support. The idea of no artillery availability was worrisome. This was my big test. Would the guys let me down? Would I make some fatal mistake? Would I let the lieutenant and the CO (commanding officer) down? Who in the hell thought up this assignment? Why me?

We were eleven tired guys, hours away from any meaningful support, fumbling their way through hostile territory and hoping to reach a mark on a map using just compass readings, counting steps, and the skills of a simple-minded sergeant with an amusement-park background. Talk about pressure! Okay, Weitzel; you wanted to lead. Be careful what you wish for.

At one point, about midnight, we nearly ran into a bunch of VC crossing a rice paddy. They heard us and for whatever reason chose to disappear. Whew—we lucked out on that one. I about pissed in my pants.

Suddenly, about two-thirds of the way into the mission, we emerged from the light jungle vegetation into a huge clearing about the size of an elementary school campus. Here, in the middle of the jungle was this large size field of plowed earth with large clumps of dirt. "What the fuck?" I said out loud. "Where did this come from?"

I looked at the map, and it showed nothing resembling a field. I wondered if we were lost. Of course, the maps we used weren't always accurate. Even early on "in country," some officers actually used old National Geographic magazine maps because the army didn't have any current ones.

Seeing this huge, open field sent me for a loop. Had I gotten my bearings wrong? Where were we? I took out my poncho, got the flashlight, and covered myself to prevent any light leaks. I studied the map, looking for anything resembling an open field. I couldn't find anything that looked like what we were seeing. Double Fuck! I resorted to asking the guys, "What do you think? Have I gotten us lost?"

One old farm boy said, "No, Sarge, I think we're okay. This looks like a new field of some type." We had no clue why it was there, but it now created a second problem for us.

Our course was diagonally across the four hundred plus meters of open space. The terrain was going to slow us down, but worse yet, we'd be exposed if we were ambushed by a VC mortar attack. Three well-placed mortar rounds and the Third Squad would be no more! If we skirted the perimeter we'd no doubt add another forty-five minutes to our travel time and probably miss the rendezvous. Failing to complete the mission would mean a demotion back to private for me. I would have failed my big test, letting the lieutenant, captain, and Third Squad down.

Why a furrowed field of this size in the middle of the jungle? Was it a VC trap? Should we skirt or cross it? I wrestled with those questions and more. I had a mission to complete, but I was also responsible for ten other guys. Decisions, decisions. What seemed like five minutes of decision-making was probably just a few seconds. Leadership requires one making a decision with less than fifty percent of the needed information. Time was wasting; it was nearly 2:30 A.M., and we still had another three thousand or so meters to travel if we were on the right course and not lost! The guys were offering their suggestions, but the ultimate decision rested with the simple-minded sergeant with an amusement park background.

The words of Lieutenant Walker were echoing in my head. *"This is a critical mission. You've got to be at the L.Z. by 0500 hours. Now move 'em out."*

"Okay guys," I said. "We cross as quickly as we can haul our tired asses to the other side. Tally-Ho Green." Man, that four hundred meter expanse loomed large as we started across. At any moment I was expecting to hear AK-47 or mortar rounds raining down on us.

After thirty minutes of difficult and tiresome traveling over large clumps of plowed earth, we reached the relative safety of jungle covering on the other side. Whew! Dumb luck.

The terrain was brutal. The packs (rucksacks) got heavier and heavier, and our feet slower and slower, but we pushed on without complaints. I knew the guys were more tired than I was, but they kept moving. What else could we do? We had a mission, and once we were past the point of no return (that never entered our minds), we had to move forward. The guys did well. I did not have to worry about them. I was concerned about me, dog-tired, leading the way, and trying to hold the whole thing together.

The rest of the trek was uneventful except for a couple of water buffalo humping each other in the bushes.

Somehow, we reached our destination about 5:15 A.M. and secured the LZ. The sun was coming up over the jungle canopy. The radio crackled; we heard the inbound choppers calling for us to identify ourselves and marking smoke (grenades). We tossed several smokes and waited as twenty-six Hueys came swooping into the area carrying our company—Charlie. They immediately took up a defensive perimeter, and a few minutes later came the artillery choppers with 88s and 105s slung from their underbellies. Lieutenant Walker congratulated and thanked the squad for a successful mission. Not only did we look good, but also, he had passed his first leadership assignment. His platoon/squad had not let him (or the company commander) down. We tried to rest and sleep for the next few hours, but all the noise, activity, and movement made it nearly impossible. Those artillery guys were sighting and test firing their big guns—loud!

About 10:00 A.M., in came the tank-mounted 155 mm big guns. By afternoon, our company was on the move again, this time replaced by Delta Company. They looked refreshed. It seemed that Charlie Company was always on the move. I often wondered why that was. A few days later I was promoted to platoon sergeant and told by Lieutenant Walker that the company commander had requested me specifically for the LZ mission. I was told that he knew if anyone could accomplish such a squad mission (that required speed), it would be me. If true, this was a nice compliment. For that and other outstanding performance I was later awarded the Army Commendation Medal; the army's eighth-highest decoration.

SENSE OF TIME

By that time, most of us were past the halfway point in our thirteen-month tour in Vietnam. We had become battle-hardened, jungle-savvy, fearless fighters. We were of a different mindset than we had been six months earlier. Individually and as a unit, we were a well-oiled fighting machine. We had lost almost all sense of time. We might know the month but certainly not the day or date. Time flowed from one mission to another; we were always on the move. In some ways we preferred it that way. As strangers in a foreign land, fighting an elusive enemy, and humping it through the jungle, we had plenty of time with our own thoughts. That was dangerous, of course, because if we did not stay alert, old Charlie would smoke our young asses. Even so, it was hard staying focused minute to minute, and often times we would be moving through the jungle but transported to a different place and time by our wandering thoughts of a different life. We had adapted to the world of jungle warfare. Our senses were alert to danger even if we were not conscious of it. Oh, we had had some narrow escapes and reminders to stay sharp, but the endless trudging through thick jungle tended to pull our thoughts to other realms. Yes, we had learned the rules of the jungle and jungle warfare. We truly were God's Lunatics!

NIGHT AMBUSH—HOT FIREFIGHT

After the mission to secure the artillery-landing zone, Lieutenant Walker and I really bonded. As platoon sergeant, I started spending more time with him. The Third Squad was taken over by Corporal Farmer. The platoon was realigned. Some guys rotated out to other units, we had a couple of guys killed and wounded in the Niagara Falls and Junction City firefights, and the six-month round of promotions changed our makeup as well.

As Junction City wound down, the battalion started moving toward the Cambodian border and the Ho Chi Minh Trail, which moved in and out of Vietnam and Cambodia. The Viet Cong were bringing down lots of supplies from North Vietnam. It was later learned that this was in preparation for the Tet Offensive, which began January 7, 1968.

We were fighting in the Viet Cong's home territory. Even though the war was about freeing South Vietnam from the tentacles of the Communist North, many of the citizens were sympathetic to the North and supported their efforts to rout the Americans from their land. We never knew if the Vietnamese who we were engaging were friend or foe. They might be nice, pleasant, and polite peasant farmers by day but warriors by night.

The company and our platoon had several brief encounters with the Viet Cong as they carried supplies of rice, ammunition, and weapons down this series of jungle trails. One night, the lieutenant was given orders to set up a major night ambush along a suspected VC trail. It was not unusual to have a squad of ten guys set up for an ambush, but a whole-platoon ambush involved much more planning and preparation.

Ambushes by nature are supposed to be quiet maneuvers, but with forty-two guys strung out along a trail at night, it is generally not a quiet slumber party.

Since the lieutenant seemed to be impressed with my leadership and combat skills, he pretty much let me set up the platoon in the offensive positions. We had selected a good spot along the trail, and I set about putting the squads into position, with the machine gunner in a key location. I had good flank and rear coverage as well. We had practiced this in AIT.

103

Remember, Lieutenant Walker was fresh from West Point, and although textbook smart, he had not seen much actual combat. When he surveyed the setup, he was quite impressed. That made me proud and proved a good strategic move later that night, when all hell broke loose. I settled in toward the center of the line, and the good lieutenant took a position near the upper end. Much of the night was quiet. It was a half moon, and the jungle vegetation was not terribly thick. It was nearly a perfect night and situation for an ambush.

Along about 2:00 A.M., the jungle sounds suddenly became still. Something electric filled the air, and suddenly we were all alert. Our senses had picked up something. Dead calm for a few moments, and then we heard the faint rustle of vegetation and movement. Some "thing" was coming down the trail.

We had set up about a dozen feet off the foot-worn trail. Guys were spaced in pairs, about eight feet apart, with flanking positions well covered; four pairs of guys faced rearward to protect us from any surprise encounter. The M-60 machine gunner had a good field of fire that covered nearly the entire ambush site. We had Claymore mines surrounding our position as a good defensive tactic, and the riflemen had good camouflaged positions with excellent fields of fire. It was a truly classic, textbook setup.

Nobody needed to be told to be alert. The sounds and movement were becoming more distinct and closer. Our heartbeats quickened. Each man readied himself and his weapon. Then we saw a string of dark figures moving along the trail just feet from our weapons. They were not talking, just steadily moving along, stretched out for some fifty or sixty feet, about twenty-five of them.

Suddenly a trip flare fired off, and everyone opened up a blaze of firepower. Training dictated that we hit the enemy hard and fast in a hail of bullets. Our red tracer rounds were zinging from behind our camouflaged positions, and they were met with yells, screams, and people running. The surprise had worked. The goal was to kill everyone. Sorry! War is a nasty and disgusting endeavor. It is surprising that we killed only three and not more. VC and civilians had scattered into the jungle when that first flare ignited. The whole thing must have lasted all of fifteen or twenty seconds.

We received some returning fire from the VC, but it was light. The people had scattered down the trail and into the jungle. When the firing stopped, we heard moans, cries, and wails. The lieutenant and several guys started moving out to check the damage. I placed guard units a few yards down each end of the trail in case the VC decided to return.

As we inspected our deed, we found that we had ambushed a Viet Cong group, but we had also killed and injured several civilians whom the VC had spaced within their column. We had killed two VC and one civilian. Several others were injured, but none of us had been severely hurt. One guy had a scratch on his cheek, and another had a cut and injured hand. The ambush was a success, and the intelligence had been accurate. We did our jobs and completed our mission with textbook precision; however, we had only a 10-percent kill ratio.

The quiet jungle was now full of noise, cries, and sadness. It is one thing to engage the enemy in combat but quite another to kill and maim innocent civilians. Many of us felt bad. We tended to the injured and covered up the dead with ponchos.

How many VC had been in the group? We didn't know. The whole group could have been Viet Cong or just a few of them, with the rest being civilians.

The lieutenant radioed the news to the company commander, who apparently was pleased with our success. We asked for a medical dust-off for the wounded, but that was denied until first light, which was a couple hours away.

The time went by quickly, and soon first light came. We gathered up the injured and dead, and as the helicopters came in, we loaded up the people. One VC had American dollars in his black pajamas. How he had gotten American dollars was a mystery, as we were all paid in Vietnamese piastres.

The battalion and company commanders came out to inspect the situation. We never learned if the civilians had been forced from some village and made to travel with the VC or if they were family members.

After the commanders departed, we gathered up our gear and hoofed it to our next mission. It was a somber day. We had done our job and done it well, but the reality of our deed had had a profound effect on us.

The smells, sights, and sounds of death touch one's soul in a profoundly haunting way. People who have had a significant emotional encounter in life rarely talk about it. They may mention it, but seldom do they open themselves up for outside examination. It is something personal, deep, and private.

"War is corrosive of human nature and the good society." – Aristotle

THE FALLEN SEVEN

That chapter in our thirteen months in Vietnam stayed with us for a long time, and for many of us it is still a vivid, haunting memory. Niagara Falls and Junction City had kept us in the field for seventy-seven days. It had been a turning point in our lives. We had stared death in the face, and it had ridden on our shoulders. For some, the door to another world had opened, and they had entered, never to return to Earth. We went back to Camp Bearcat for much-needed rest—emotionally and physically—and to clean our gear. We spent a good week showering, cleaning our weapons, and generally unwinding from our tight emotional strains. We had not realized it out in the field, but we were nearing the breaking point. Fortunately, our commanders had recognized the signs.

It was a quiet week of recuperation. We were able to sleep in each day until about 7:00 A.M. Chow was hot and tasty, and any time we wanted, we could use the showers—and they were hot. Discipline and routine were somewhat relaxed. Yes, we had to clean and regroup, but we did so at our own pace. That was good—we needed the break.

After a week of gathering our wits, we were informed that we would be having a company ceremony for the seven comrades who had been killed during the Niagara and Junction City operations. After morning chow, we were instructed to get our rifles and fall into formation for a memorial service. Now we knew that the military is big on ceremony, decorations, and honors, but this simple act was more touching than all the parades, pomp, and circumstance seen by the public. On the red Vietnamese earth stood seven pairs of boots lined up in front of seven M-16 rifles, bayonet down in the earth, each topped with the soldier's battered helmet. Behind the somber row was the battalion chaplain with a purple cloth and bible in hand. It was a simple yet elegant tribute to our fallen brethren. We all had known some of the fallen soldiers, but I somehow could not put clear images of the faces to the names being read off. I wondered if this was how it was. Did facial recognition fade so quickly after a person dies? At age twenty-three, I had not had a lot of experience with death. Oh, I remembered the faces of my grandparents, but was this how it was for people whom one did not know on a sustained basis? The ceremony deeply touched each of us. I think we all had watery eyes—including our commanders.

Boots, rifle, and a helmet—A vivid tribute and memory.

THE BLACK VIRGIN

The next operation was a wet one. It was Operation Junction City II. The rains had turned the operational area into a muddy bog. We were headed to an area that would become quite interesting—the Black Virgin Mountain (if you can call it a mountain). We conducted some typical search-and-destroy missions and then were assigned as firebase protection for an artillery group. What we did not realize was that we would be helping to dig out buried tanks and retrieval vehicles.

Our sandbag bunkers were ankle deep in water all the time, and sleeping was none too comfortable. The monsoons had turned the flat plains into a swamp. Tanks, tractors, trucks, and even personnel were deeply buried and stuck in the muck. Rising out of this mess was the lonely Black Virgin Mountain, which looked oddly out of place. Much of our time was spent digging out the mud in and around stuck and buried vehicles so that they could be towed out of their graves. It is difficult to decide which operation was more demanding—fighting Charlie in his natural element of the jungle or fighting Mother Nature, the rain, and mud of the Black Virgin Mountain region.

We spent our nights pulling guard duty and our days helping dig out heavy equipment. How does a tank commander tell his captain, "Oops, Sir. I buried my tank in five feet of mud!" Even the tank retrievers, which are just oversize M-60 tanks with a large crane replacing the gun barrel, got stuck in the mud and had to be pulled out by a team of tractors. Trucks, those deuce-and-a-halfs (two-and-a-half-ton) were going nowhere, and they had four-wheel drive. Want to stop an army? Mother Nature did with all that mud.

My bunker (a foxhole fortified with sandbags around the side and top to provide protection from artillery or mortar fire) was at the entrance of the artillery base camp, which afforded me a good view of the stuck-in-the-mud problems the tankers were facing.

C-130

We usually did not stay in any one place very long, and that was true for the Black Virgin Mountain. After a few days of firebase guard duty and digging out tanks, we were ready for our next mission. By then we were pinballing all around the Third Corp's area of operation, but this time we were being sent to help the 25th Division in the First Corp's area, up north.

About the second day, three big C-130 transport planes landed, and a couple of hours later we were formed up as a company (164 men) and were marched across the field to begin boarding these cavernous beasts. The back loading ramps were down, and we filed on in two columns on either side of the huge belly of the plane, which had already been loaded with Jeeps, boxes of C-rations, crates of ammunition, and cold-weather jackets. We got ourselves seated on web slings, which folded down and were attached to the sides of the aluminum airframe. The crew chief asked us to unload and clear our weapons. I guess he did not want anyone of God's Lunatics shooting holes in his aircraft. Silly crew chief! We know that there were no banana leafs or boa constrictors on a C-130. Right, Weitzel, and Fitzwater?

As we were sitting, M-16s between our knees, we were wondering where we were off to next. Not that it really mattered. After all, one got used to not knowing the intended destination—we were just along for the free ride. If you don't know where you're going, then any path will take you there, to paraphrase the Cheshire Cat's conversation with Alice. Now in case you have not yet understood, it is damn hot and humid in Vietnam—I mean hell hot!

So, as we were riding along inside this huge cargo plane loaded with men and material, we were wondering to ourselves why in the hell the plane was loaded with cold-weather field jackets. Did the army fuck up again? Well, we were about to find out. About an hour into the flight, the CO came onto the PA and announced that we had been assigned to assist the 25th Division. Our battalion, the 4th, some 900 men, was going to be pushing the VC into a "net" set up by the 25th. (Now why the 25th could not do that itself was not for me to ask, but here we come. Leave it up to the Old Reliables again.)

And, oh, by the way, we were headed for Pleiku, up north, where it was hot during the day and cold at night. Cold, hell—that was an understatement. It turned out to be freezing! It was 70 degrees at night. Don't laugh—that is damn cold after having been in 100-degree weather for nine months and your blood has thinned. Even those heavy jackets that we used in 22-degree weather back on the cold Kansas plains were not bulky enough to keep us warm in Pleiku.

Our support mission to assist the 25th in Pleiku was uneventful for us. We were in the region for four or five days, conducted several patrols, but saw no enemy activity. We eventually moved on to another assignment.

"I'M GONNA DIE!"

For some reason, I seemed to have just as much trouble with Vietnam's fauna and flora as I did the enemy. One night we set up in a defensive position in some bunkers, having moved into the position late at night, around 9:00 P.M. The night was black—no moon—so we sort of stumbled around, trying to get situated. As normal, we took shifts doing guard duty. My turn came around, and I was sitting on top of the bunker's sand bags, my feet dangling into the foxhole and arms resting on the roof. My M-16 was nearby. I do not remember what I was thinking of, probably daydreaming of life after Vietnam. Suddenly I felt a biting sting on my finger, which instantly caused me to throw up my arm. A second later, more-intense pain grabbed my chest, and I felt an instant crushing vice grip squeezing me. *I'm gonna die!* was my thought. I did not know what had happened, but I jumped from the foxhole and started stumbling my way toward the medic's location. Hell, I didn't know where to go! We had been lucky to have gotten our guys situated in the dark, but I had no idea where to find the medic. My chest muscles were constricting tighter and tighter as I labored to breathe. I stumbled over guys, who cursed me out. I asked directions as I fumbled in the dark and somehow located the medic's foxhole.

"Doc, Doc—I'm dying!"

"What's wrong?"

"I don't know. Something must have stung me. My finger and chest are numb, and I feel like there's a ton of bricks on my chest. I can't breathe. I'm gonna die!" Without even looking at my "wounds" he told me that probably a scorpion had stung me and that I would be okay. "Go back to your foxhole; the numbness will go away soon." Bastard! I was dying!

The military blouses we wore were loose fitting for better ventilation. We would often have them unbuttoned and hanging loose as we traveled through the countryside. What probably had happened was that when I was stung on the finger by the scorpion, my reactionary arm motion flung him onto my chest and down my open and loose blouse, where it stung me in the chest. Damn scorpion!

111

As I tried to find my way back to my bunker, I began to wonder where in the hell that damn scorpion was. It was dark, remember; no moon! Was he still in or around the bunker? Did he have pals with him? Did I dare sit down? Hell, they had never trained us on how to deal with scorpions, snakes, or banana leaves. The tightness seemed to last for a long time, especially sitting in the dark, but it was probably only twenty or thirty minutes. I do not think I even woke up my bunker mate for his watch turn because I was too concerned about other scorpions coming to get me. Thinking back on all of this some forty years later, I think I was more afraid of the scorpions, snakes, and fire ants than I was of the enemy. Sure, the adrenalin pumps when you're in a firefight, but you do not realize the danger or fear it. However, I was fearful of the creepy crawlers lurking around the area.

Another time, I had put my helmet on the ground while I was shaving. When I put my helmet on, I felt something crawling on my head. I threw off my helmet and brushed my head, and a huge scorpion, stinger at the ready, hit the ground. It scared the living hell out of me, but I escaped injury that time!

THE SWIMMING ARMORED
PERSONNEL CARRIER

We moved to the Mekong Delta[6] and worked in the mangrove swamps, where the tree roots love the water and grow branches that spread and send down more roots, thus forming more trunks and causing a thick growth over a large area. It is hard travel having to step over the protruding roots and navigate through the thick growth. Of course, one's feet are always wet. And, the soldier had better watch out for the water moccasin snakes.

One day, we had the fortunate opportunity to do a sweep of a large area by riding on armored personnel carriers (APCs). Like large SUVs, these tread-driven vehicles carried about ten fully loaded GIs inside their belly and two or three more on top. Each squad loaded into and on an APC. I just happened to be sitting on top, and our carrier was in the point position of a V formation. We were traveling through a watery plain at a pretty good clip, just trying to hold on and not fall off. I think that the APC drivers liked to show off and jostle their passengers. All of a sudden, our carrier's nose dove down and went underwater. Okay, I did not remember anything like this in my training. Of course the machine gunner on the carrier was holding on; he was okay, but the driver was submerged and water flooded inside. The other grunt and I on top were nearly washed off. Here was another incident "in country" that scared the blue blazes out of me. We were loaded down with our rucksacks, gear, and machine gun ammo. Luckily, we bobbed to the surface, soaking wet, but that was okay—we were used to being wet. Surprise! The damn thing floats. The waterline is about six inches from the top of the carrier, but with its rubber flaps along the track treads, it creates locomotion for water travel. We managed to navigate what was a flooded river, and we reached the opposite bank, where the carrier climbed out and onto higher ground. People think that

---

6 The Mekong Delta (Vietnamese: "Nine Dragon River Delta") is the region in southwestern Vietnam where the Mekong River approaches and empties into the sea through a network of tributaries. The Mekong Delta encompasses a large portion of southeastern Vietnam, about 39,000 square kilometers. The size of the area covered by water depends on the season. —*Wikipedia.*

113

infantrymen are crazy, but I am telling you that tankers, helicopter pilots, and APC drivers are the true lunatics.

SANTA FE, ON MY WAY

Time was marching on, and we were now beginning Operation Santa Fe. We were back to our routine of search-and-destroy missions, finding and blowing up tunnels, and playing tag with the Viet Cong—Tag; You're it. I knew I was getting close to the end of my tour of duty in Vietnam, but I did not know the exact date. In fact, I did not know what month it was. We were truly out of touch with the outside world. We were in the jungle and had just set up camp for the night. It had been a long day, not unlike many others. The helicopters were landing and unloading supplies. I had my poncho and gear spread out and was starting to open a can of C-rations, using a P-38 can opener that I always carried in my helmet camouflage band. The lieutenant called over to me and said, "Weitzel, your tour of duty is up. You're out of here. That's your helicopter ride out of here, and it's leaving in thirty seconds!"

As he was saying that, the last helicopter was revving up its engine to take off. Those guys did not like to sit on the ground any longer than was necessary. I grabbed my poncho, rucksack, and rifle and ran to that chopper. I did not say goodbye to anyone, including Lieutenant Walker, who I greatly admired. As I reached the chopper, it was already a few inches off the ground. I threw my stuff onto the floor and scrambled aboard. It must have been a funny sight to those watching. If I had not gotten aboard that last chopper, no telling when the next time I would have had a chance to get a ride out.

The chopper was loaded with outbound supplies and one other fella headed to Camp Bearcat. This guy and the two door gunners looked at me as if I was crazy. There I was, sitting on the floorboard of this outbound Huey, heading for what I thought was Bearcat. Oh, no! I learned that we were headed for a base some 200 miles from Bearcat. When we landed, and I do not recall where, it was at a chopper base where they were not equipped to handle guys coming in from the field. Some chopper pilots did transport, some flew medivacs, others flew gunships, and some flew observation. These guys were not too happy about having a stinking, and I mean stinking, ground-pounder in their chopper. Upon landing, we were told to check in with the dispatcher, far across the tarmac. So, this other guy and I head for the communications hut. It was getting late. The sun was setting, and things at this base camp were buttoning up for the day.

When we found the dispatcher, he was not too impressed. We were stinking GIs, dirty, fully loaded with rifles, ammunition, grenades, gear, and mud, standing in his nice, clean office. We told the unhappy dispatcher that we were headed for Bearcat, but he said that there were no flights out that night; we would have to check in the next morning. Maybe then we could catch a flight to another camp and hopscotch our way to Bearcat. Here we were, tired, carrying our rifles, explosives, hand and smoke grenades, Claymore mines, plastic explosives, field telephones, rucksacks, and half the dirt in Vietnam on our persons. The dispatcher was not much help. He was a young kid, and this situation was new to him. He did not know how to deal with Cong Killers. When we asked him where we could get some chow, clean up, and bunk down for the night, he was thrown for a loop; he simply did not know.

The two of us found a deuce-and-a-half near the chopper field and bedded down in the back of it. We opened our C-rations and ate cold ham and lima beans. We found a nearby latrine but no shower. Yep, jungle fighters can make do under Spartan conditions. We were awake at first light, ate some rations, and headed for the dispatch office, which thankfully opened at 6:00 A.M. We checked in with the new dispatcher and told him our tale of woe. A flight was headed out for a nearby camp, but we would have to check with the chopper pilot to see if we could catch a ride. We checked. The pilot was reluctant—we stunk to high heaven—but he agreed to give us a lift. Much appreciated.

At the next hopscotch stop, we again had to wait several hours for a chopper going to Bearcat, but we caught one in the late afternoon and got to Bearcat in the late evening. The other fella and I parted, and I started walking the three miles (with gear—no big deal) toward the unit's camp. An E-4 (corporal) driving a jeep stopped and asked where I was headed. He offered me a much-appreciated lift.

The camp was pretty much deserted. Everyone was in the field except one office clerk and a supply sergeant. I got a quick, cold shower, found a bunk, and crashed. I did not sleep too well. The next morning I found an open mess hall for breakfast and waited for the supply and office clerks to open the office. I checked in and got the papers and instructions necessary to rotate out of the unit. I could not turn my gear into the supply sergeant but had to lug it down to the central mustering-out location. I spent several hours cleaning my rifle, webbing, and gear. I gathered it and hauled it to the specified location. When I got there, the line was long. I asked a few questions of those waiting and found out my next step. A little after 3:00 in the afternoon they announced that the station would be closing at 4:00 P.M. and we would need to come back the next day. We were reminded that all gear needed to be clean. I hiked back to camp, got a hot meal, and started to reclean my stuff. There was really nothing else to do. Heavily used combat gear gets very dirty, worn, and tattered. I had my M-16 with me all through training as well as through my twelve months of intense jungle combat. Overall, my trusty M-16 had been by my side, every day, for nineteen months.

I was in line at 8:00 A.M. the next morning. The sergeant called out that anyone past his rotation date was to move to the front of the line. My papers showed that I had been kept out in the field six days past my rotation date, and I was a total of nine days beyond my rotation date out. I moved up to second in line. The sergeant checked my orders and then directed me to the first check-in spot to turn in my rifle. Six or eight check-in stations were inside this huge tent. Each station received a particular level of returns. Uniforms only were one aisle. Uniforms and web gear was another. A third aisle for soldiers with a weapon, web gear, and uniforms, and a special line for us Cong Killers. It was a long aisle for those of us lugging around half of the army's light weapons, ammunition, and equipment. Big bins behind each station stop were for the various articles: rifle, ammunition, grenades (smoke, concussion, fragmentation), mines (Claymore), flares, M-60 rounds, webbing, rucksack, trenching tool, bayonet, sandbags, flashlight, compass, field radio, food, plastic explosive, first-aid supplies, Class C (fatigues) uniform, Class B (khaki), Class A (dress), ropes, and assorted other equipment we carried around for 365 days.

Everything we were issued in training, for combat, and personal items had to be turned in. We could take nothing except one Class B uniform out of country. They stripped us bare; except for the clothes on our backs. Most of the guys waiting in line were not combat GIs. Remember, only one in eleven GIs was a combat soldier, and that could be armor, artillery, or infantry. The other ten were clerks, cooks, drivers, mechanics, medics, laundry, supply, personnel, or members of a host of other support units. Their clothes and equipment were almost brand new. They got laundry service and three square meals a day. Here I was, lean, mean, tan, dirty (the soil sunk into your pores), and a combat-hardened buck sergeant. Our types are not much for talking! The fair-skinned, starched, uniformed private behind the counter took my M-16 and gave me an inquisitive look. He checked the rifle and said to me, "This weapon isn't clean. It's pitted, and the bluing is worn off. I can't accept it in this condition."

I saw red and I tore into this young private!

"What in the fuck do you think it's going to look like after being fired thousands of times over twelve months in the muck and mud I've been living in? While you've been sitting in a clean office, fucking mama-san, I've been out in the fucking jungle protecting your young ass. This rifle is as clean as it is going to get. You either take it or I'll shove it up your dirty ass!"

Whoa! Everyone within a thirty-foot radius got deathly quiet. The private turned white and glanced over at the young lieutenant who was quietly standing off to one side, supervising the operation. This young officer could not have been more than twenty and was obviously new "in country" and not at all combat hardened like the crazy sergeant with a worn M-16. He was probably thinking to himself, "This guy is ready to snap. He has an M-16 and a chest full of grenades, and I don't even have my .45; better not mess with this crazy sarge." The lieutenant nodded his head in acceptance, and the private took my weapon and hastily signed off on my release form and handed it back to me, without checking any more of my gear.

Boy, did I move quickly down the entire check-in line without any further problems. Nobody even bothered to inspect my stuff. They just took my equipment, initialed the proper spot on my paperwork as fast as they could, and tossed me my release form. I must have finished in record time.

The reader should know that the 9th Division was formed, trained, and shipped to Vietnam as a unit. Those of us turning in our gear had all trained and fought together. The new lieutenant and private were probably new to the army and the 9th Division. We had been issued the equipment (webbing, rifle, trenching tool, bayonet, and assorted gear) twenty months earlier in basic training, and we had used it all the time during our tour of duty. No way was any of that equipment ever going to look brand new. Clean? Hell! They were lucky if any of it was still usable. It was torn, ripped, worn, and imbedded with dirt, mud, and gunk. Here they were telling me how my equipment and gear was supposed to look when they had no idea of what we had been through during those past twenty months. It was a classic case of the young bear cub trying to tell the papa grizzly about survival in the forest. Yeah, right! That little snot nosed, pale-faced private just out of boot camp had no idea of the horrific jungle conditions we endured, but he sure learned a lesson about challenging buck sergeants!

I guess being "loaded for bear" with hand grenades, C-4 plastic explosive, Claymore mines, and a bandolier full of M-60 rounds made some lasting impression on all the GIs who had witnessed this affair. Most of them probably hadn't seen (let alone used) any of this gear since basic training. I think that at that point, everyone in the area—and the army in general—wanted to get the crazy sergeant out as fast as they could. I had my "Get-Out-Of-Jail-Free" card stamped, and nobody wanted anything to do with me at that point. Even the MPs at the end of the line who patted me (and everyone else) down were quick at their task. No flags, weapons, maps, or hidden contraband. "That worked," I said to myself as I headed for my physical clearance and personnel sign-offs. One gets a little cocky wearing a CIB. If rifle bullets coming at you could not intimidate you, not much else could.

Four days after returning to Bearcat, I was cleared to rotate out to the transportation center, where I had to wait on standby until a spot became available. Since I had missed my initial date, I was back at the bottom of the list, so I had to wait about three days. The chow was good, but there was nothing much to do. No theaters or recreation areas. I just had to sit waiting each hour for my name to be called. Boring.

When the time came to leave, we boarded a bus to the Bien Hoa airbase, where we waited in a large, open-air hanger for our "freedom bird" to arrive. We were still in a combat zone, so it was common for the VC to lob in a few mortars from outlying areas. As the big bird came in, it taxied to a spot away from the waiting area. They did not shut down the engines— just in case they needed a hasty exit. The doors opened, and, like a ton of bricks, the blast of hot, humid air hit the disembarking recruits.

These new arrivals had no idea what was in store for them; you could see it in their pale faces. No sooner were they off the plane than we boarded; we were airborne in twenty minutes. As we lifted off, a loud cheer erupted from the 200 thankful GIs. We were on our twenty-one-hour journey, via Alaska, home. We went the polar route from Southeast Asia to Oakland, California, a longer but faster route due to the earth's curvature.

We refueled at Anchorage at 2:00 A.M. Now remember, this was in 1967. It was a small airport then, and we had to disembark and walk outside to the terminal. Here we were, 200 GIs in short-sleeved shirts, coming from 100-plus degree heat into an environment of snow and zero degrees. Now it was time for our weather shock.

When we landed at the Oakland Naval Air Station, we were escorted into an area to be checked in and given our new orders. We were searched. We had not been allowed to bring anything from Vietnam other than the uniform we wore. All gear, personal items, and anything else had to be left in Vietnam. How some guys managed to sneak out flags, grenades, or weapons is beyond me.

While we were getting the paperwork and inspections completed, in another room, some twenty seamstresses were busy sewing on unit patches, attaching ribbons, and adorning our Class A uniforms with the proper military garnishments. These ladies were fast! We probably waited fifteen or twenty minutes in the holding area before our names were called and the sharp, new, crisp uniforms and caps were issued to us. It made us feel proud. Here were all of our current decorations, awards, and insignia. It was the first time we had seen the recognition of our efforts over the past twenty months. In the dressing room, we stood in front of the full-length mirrors and admired our impressive appearance. Lean, tan, and full of decorations. Wow, the girls back home would be impressed. (And how about the ladies of the evening waiting just outside, as the newly arrived soldiers exited the building?) One final inspection by an officer, then we were given our thirty-day leave money and a transportation voucher good for a one-way trip to anywhere in the United States, and then one way to our next duty assignment. I think I got about $115 in pay, one month's worth. It did not include the $10 per month hazard-duty pay that I received while "in country."

We were checked to ensure we had orders, voucher, and pay in hand, and then we were released. Hot meals were available, but most of us just grabbed a sandwich and went our separate ways. A string of taxis waited outside to take us wherever we wanted. My driver offered to drive me to San Jose for $165—a special deal for us veterans. Yeah, right!

At the Oakland bus depot, the ticketing agent saw me take my wallet out of a plastic liner (used to keep things "dry" in the humid Vietnam climate). She cautioned me to be careful, as someone might want to mug me for my thirty days' pay. *Let 'em try* was my thought. I was not a big fella and maybe not "Superman" strong, but boy, I knew how to kill with my hands, and I was in a tightly wrapped survival mode. It would have been a fair fight, but the muggers would probably have come out on the short end of that deal.

People on the bus gave me strange and long looks during the seventy-minute ride to San Jose. I did not realize at the time, having been out of the loop for over a year, that antiwar sentiment was running strong in the States. Many protest marches were taking place, and the upcoming Democratic Convention in July 1968 would be riotous.

They could probably tell by my general appearance that I was just back from the war. They did not bother to talk to me, and that was fine with me. Our type was not much for talking. The taxi driver who brought me home from the bus depot tried to engage me in conversation, but I was silent, just taking in the scenery. What a contrast. We Americans take so much for granted. Mom, Dad, and Allen were not home when I arrived, and I had no way of contacting them, so I decided to surprise them.

I waited on the backyard patio until they came home. I gave them a few minutes to get settled in and went around the front to ring the doorbell. Mom just stood in the doorway, looking at me for the longest time. I think she was in mild shock. Then she started to tear up; the biggest smile came to her face, and she finally opened the screen door. Dad, too, was happy to see me, but in a reserved and military manner. He told me he was glad I was home safe and sound.

Allen had the most outward expression of gladness. When he came home, I was sitting at the dining room table. Allen walked in wearing his red Frontier Village Amusement Park uniform shirt and black cowboy hat. He stopped in his tracks and just looked at me, and then he gave me a hug for the longest time. He looked great. Trim, matured, and no longer the baby brother I had remembered from two years before.

Dinner that night was awkward. I knew what had happened over the past couple of years because of all the family letters, but Mom, Dad, and Allen did not ask me about my year away. I am sure that they saw a big change in me, and I noticed their stares and glances as we silently ate our first meal together in fourteen months.

Had the world changed? Had I changed? A little of both?

WE NEVER DISCUSSED IT

As a family, we never discussed our political views on the war. Allen and I were probably too young to have any definite perspective, and Mom and Dad generally did not talk politics.

I have been asked how the family felt about my going to Vietnam. Again, that was never really discussed. I think Dad was proud of me. Of course, he was concerned for my safety, but through me, he was living a dream that he had missed as a World War II marine sniper. He spent much of that war stationed in Hawaii as the generals' carpenter and rifle instructor; he never got a chance to use his sniper training and skills in the South Pacific. Published stories abound about Paul Weitzel's expert rifleman skills in hitting the butt end of a peanut from 100 yards and having the run of the marine base as the carpenter to the generals. Allen, the family historian, has a whole collection of Dad's many achievements and antics.

Nevertheless, at the time, we never discussed my going to Vietnam or my opinion of that war.

THE CLOCK SPRING

My thirty-day leave went by all too quickly, but that was soon to be remedied. During my leave, I tried to cram in all the things I had been thinking about during my 360-plus days in the jungle. I just didn't have enough time to live out all my dreams. Of course, Mom, Dad, and Allen had things for me to do and people to see. During my absence, Allen had taken a job at Frontier Village, the amusement park where I had been working when I was drafted, and he was heavily involved in that work, so I wanted to hear all of his stories and happenings. Seeing family and friends was difficult. Yes, they were glad to see me and vice versa, but what does one talk about to someone who has not come face-to-face with the veil of war? Only comrades who have shared mutual experiences can truly appreciate the rawness of war.

Somehow, we muddled through the awkward, reuniting moments. It must have been harder for others than it was for me. Even though I was home, I was still wound tight and ready to pounce should the senses warrant. It was not the loud noises that triggered a response, but little sounds like a door being unlocked or a twig snapping. In the jungle these are warning sounds, sounds of danger. Inwardly, I fought hard to present a "normal" mood, but I was profoundly aware that it would be some time before I could genuinely begin to relax. Some guys who came back were never fully able to assimilate into everyday society. I guess it is like learning to walk or speak again after a serious injury or illness. One has to put forth a tremendous effort to restore what the trauma had taken away.

Even now, more than forty years later, I have nightmares at times. My brother told me that he had an appreciation for my nightmares after he watched a TV series, *Tour Of Duty,* and endured several sleepless nights after each viewing. Although my nightmares are much less frequent, they return periodically, often triggered by a comment or the memory of an incident relating to the war. Usually the restless nights will last for a few days. The dreams may be about real events that I experienced, or they may be totally unrelated to my actual experiences. In one such dream I was a captain of a brown water assault craft and I ran it aground. As punishment, I was demoted two grades in rank and pay and put back in the jungle again. What was *that* dream all about? I must have had ham and lima bean C-rations for dinner.

FORT SILL, OKLAHOMA

Poof, the thirty-day leave was gone, and I was headed to my next duty assignment, the headquarters company of the 4th Army stationed at Fort Sill, Oklahoma. Talk about a soft-duty assignment. I wondered what I was going to be doing at Fort Sill, and it was a surprise when I found out. I mentioned previously that the commander had given special privileges and courtesies to combat infantrymen, such as extra portions of food, first-in-line privileges, and officers saluting CIB recipients. I checked into my unit and was told I would be working in the personnel section. My commander was a chief warrant officer, grade four. A warrant officer is skilled in a specialized area, such as personnel or payroll, motor mechanics, communications, helicopters or aircraft, medicine, or logistics. These guys know their stuff but spend all of their time in their specialized area. Unlike commissioned officers, who may rotate from field to administrative assignments, warrants stay pretty much in the same occupational slot.

My first shock came when I checked in at the company headquarters; the company clerk looked at me standing in front of his desk in my Class A uniform, a chest full of decorations topped with a CIB and two different shoulder patches. Most uniforms were worn with the unit's patch on the left shoulder, but soldiers who have seen actual combat for thirty days or more are entitled to wear their Combat Unit Patch on the right shoulder. You will not see many men or women in uniform who have two shoulder patches. The bespectacled "kid" had obviously never been face-to-face with a true warrior; he was awestruck. Here I am, lean, mean, tan, and combat-hardened, staring down at this pale-faced paper pusher. What a contrast! The military gods must have been laughing. I was given my room assignment. What a shock—a semi-private room (one other guy). During the previous twenty months I had never slept with less than twenty guys in a room. Then I was told where to report on Monday morning. What's this? You guys don't work on weekends? Shock number two. Shock number three would come on Monday!

THE ARMY HAS A PROBLEM

So, I got the rest of my uniforms—fatigues and Class B (warm-weather khakis). I reported to my CO, whose name escapes me. He was a nice but weather-beaten W-4 about to retire. I sat at his desk in this huge room filled with clerks typing away. The chief—that's how we were supposed to address him—looked over my personnel file, then looked up at me, looked back at the file, back at me, and then said, "I see here you can type."

"Yes sir."

"How fast?"

"About 60-plus words per minute before I got drafted."

"I don't know why they sent you to me," he said. "You're too valuable to be stuck here." That was the end of that discussion. He handed me a sheet of paper with twenty-five names on it and directed me to an old, manual typewriter sitting on a table just large enough to hold it. He told me to type the orders from the list onto individual order sheets; they were duty assignments for the guys stationed at Fort Sill. Many of them were going to be shipped off to Vietnam. Now where I had just come from, when given an order, you move and you move fast. Get it done! So I took the list over to the desk, found the blank forms, and set about my assignment. I may have been a little rusty as a typist but certainly not unproven. It took me about twenty-five minutes to type out those orders—about one minute per name—and that included making corrections. I checked my work, walked over to the chief, and handed it to him. He looked at me, the work, and then said, "Sit down, Sergeant. We have a problem."

Uh oh, I said to myself. What did you do wrong, Weitzel? I knew it was not my typing. I checked it. I think I used the correct forms. What could I have messed up in the first twenty-five minutes of my new assignment? The chief began. "No, sergeant; you don't understand the assignment. You see, that list of twenty-five names and the assignment of typing out their orders was to take you all day. I do not know why the army assigned you here, but I can take a pretty good guess. You see, you're a special breed. You have been in combat, and you have seen

126

and done things that most officers in this man's army have never seen or done. Most of the guys in this army have never been in combat and have no clue what fighting is all about. You have an impressive record, and you served with honor. The reports from your former commanding officers are outstanding, and you got very high marks. You are a credit to the army and yourself."

"Now, the army has a problem. You have fewer than one hundred days left in the service. The army wants and needs guys like you. They are probably hoping that by giving you a soft assignment, you'll like the duty and hopefully re-up (reenlist) for another tour of duty—six years. I'm guessing that because you can type, they assigned you here in order to convince you to stay enlisted. See? The army has a problem. What are they going to do with a hardened combat soldier like you for a hundred days?"

"Quite frankly, Sergeant, I don't know what to do with you. I have thirty clerks working for me, doing a variety of projects, and at times I'm hard pressed to keep them busy. I don't have any work for you. When I give you something, I want you to take all day doing it. I don't care what you do during the day other than you have to be here from 8:00 A.M. to 4:00 P.M., and if any other officer walks in here, you have to appear to be busy. The army doesn't know what to do with you, and quite frankly neither do I. Just look busy. Any questions?"

"No sir!"

"Okay. Dismissed."

Whoa! That blew me away. I went back to my little typing desk and just chewed on what the old chief had said. Nobody had said those things to me before. Oh, my former bosses, Joe Zukin, Ed Hutton, Keith Kittle, and Dad had all given me compliments, but compliments from a "stranger" were most enlightening.

I felt good about what the chief had told me, but I was not prepared for that turn of events. Talk about a cultural shock—from battling the elements and Viet Cong twenty hours a day, seven days a week, to twenty-five minutes of work and three good squares a day and weekends off was something for which I was unprepared.

LET'S IMPRESS THE "SHAVETAIL"

The personnel duty was nice for the first couple of weeks, but as the time wore on, it became rather boring. Oh, I would listen to the guys talk, but I didn't have much to say. A few guys would ask me about my "in-country" experiences, but I downplayed my involvement. I wanted to push those thoughts as far away as possible. On weekends I would go to the base theater and catch a movie or grab a hamburger at the NCO (Noncommissioned Officers' Club). It was nice not having to be on the go 24/7, but at times I did long for a little more activity.

About a month into my assignment, I was called to the CO's office. He was a major, and he told me that if I would reenlist for six years, the army would give me a $10,000 bonus. Back in 1968, that was a nice piece of change but not enough to turn my head from returning to my management job at Frontier Village to being a GI Joe again. I politely declined the offer.

A week later, the old chief called me to his desk and sort of fumbled for a way to tell me some "bad news." It seemed that he had to supply a sergeant for guard duty, and as much as he hated to do it, I was the only one available. He was regretful and sorry that he had to put me in that situation after all I had recently experienced, and he hoped that I would understand. I told him that it was no problem, and he seemed relieved. I later wondered if he thought I might refuse the assignment. I was actually glad that I had a little break in what was becoming a monotonous routine. Guard duty for a battalion compound involves ten to twenty soldiers being posted at various locations and being rotated every couple of hours. The job of sergeant of the guard is to keep watch over the duty soldiers.

Duty time came at 5:00 P.M. one Friday evening. I had checked the duty roster and had seen the names and ranks of the twenty guys assigned to the detail. They were milling around in a group on the parade grounds when I arrived but no sign of the officer (lieutenant) assigned as officer of the guard. I approached the group of soldiers, who looked so young and pale. Most could not have been more than nineteen or twenty, and by their lack of chest ribbons I knew that they had not been

128

in the army very long. Most were privates—maybe one or two corporals. They turned to look at this hard, tan, and battle-hardened sergeant with three rows of ribbons on his chest and a blue infantry ascot and cord topped off with a Combat Infantry Badge. They must have wondered what awaited them. After all, they were clerks, cooks, and medics, just barely out of their teens, and I was probably something they had not even seen in boot camp.

I thought to myself that this was going to be fun. I had them fall in and snap to attention. I told them my name, stated the duty assignment, and then took roll. I could see their eyes sizing me up. My snappy commands were not something they seemed accustomed to in their daily routines. At this juncture, it was well past the time the officer should have been at his assigned post, so I decided to conduct the inspection without him. As a squad leader in basic training and platoon sergeant in Vietnam, I had inspected my men hundreds of times. The inspections were not formal officer-type inspections, but I had been through them myself enough times to know how they were to be conducted, so inspecting these young troops was a breeze.

Now, guard duty inspections are precision affairs. A soldier's appearance, bearing, and weapon are all on display. Most of these guys probably had not done much guard duty since basic training, so I was going to give them a sampling of how the real army operated. Where was that darn lieutenant? Oh, well. The soldiers were formed into two squads of ten men each. The job of the officer (in this case me) was to stand in front of each man and thoroughly inspect him from head to toe, giving a most critical eye to each detail: uniform, bearing (posture and stance), and weapon. The final step is weapons inspection. Guard duty and the accompanying inspections are designed to reinforce regimented discipline.

The soldiers were posted outside building entrances and walked around weapons and ammunitions sheds, or patrolled a perimeter of a compound. The idea was to show a presence at such locations to keep others from entering. The soldier may or may not have loaded rounds in his weapon. Most of the time, the weapons were not loaded nor did the soldier have live rounds, the exception being an experienced Military Police guard at the entrance to a base or strategic (ammunition dump) location.

Our Dad told us the story of when he was in the marines during World War II. He and a friend returned to base after curfew and walked right past the guard without stopping. Dad probably knew the guard's weapon was not loaded. Dad also joked to his buddy that the guard had been a student on Dad's rifle range. The guard was a lousy shot and could not "hit the broad side of a barn."

I noted some irregularity with each man—a spot missed shaving, gig line (shirt buttons, belt buckle, and pants zipper not aligned), or dirty weapon. If they were trying to test the old sergeant, now age twenty-four, they were in for a surprise!

I never rejected a soldier for being unfit for guard duty, but if a soldier was unprepared, he was given a demerit, sent back to his unit, and disciplined by the platoon lieutenant or company commander (captain). Being unfit for any duty was not a pleasant experience; the punishment was worse than the effort of being fit for duty: thirty days of K.P. or cleaning latrines for thirty days, standing outside all night and reciting the general orders to a tree, or doing physical training (running, exercises, push-ups) while others were sleeping. Oh no—it's best not to be unfit for any duty, especially guard duty.

About halfway through the inspection, the officer showed up. He was the youngest- looking lieutenant I had ever seen, and he did not have but one or two ribbons on his chest. *Okay,* I said to myself. *Let me put him through his paces as well.* I halted my inspection and reported to him. Upon seeing my Combat Infantry Badge, he initiated the salute. He eyes fell upon to my chest of ribbons—the CIB and Army Commendation Medal. I can tell that he, too, had not had much contact with seasoned combat soldiers. He stared at my ribbons for the longest time. I imagined he was trying to mentally reconstruct my military history. I told him that the detail (guard duty) was present and accounted for, and asked him if he wanted to finish the inspection. "You carry on, Sergeant," was his reply.

"Yes, sir," was my snappy reply. One of the critical details of an inspection is when the officer (or, in this case, sergeant) reaches to take the weapon (in this case a heavy, eleven-pound M-14) out of a soldier's hands, the soldier is supposed to release the rifle just as the officer grabs it. The weapon should hang in the air for just a fraction of a second, and there should be a sharp slapping noise as the officer grabs it. If the soldier holds on too long or releases too quickly, the weapon transfer will be bungled. It is a test to see if the soldier is alert and quick.

A good officer (or seasoned infantry platoon sergeant) will try a variety of "tricks" to test the "trembling" soldier. One trick is to stand facing the soldier, look him in the eye, and then with a fast, snappy response, grab the weapon. Quickness by both parties is the key. I could see out of the corner of my eye that the young lieutenant was intensely watching as I moved down the line, snatching weapons, thoroughly inspecting them, and smartly returning them. It was an impressive technique that I had learned from Captain Risor in basic training. He was one for precision and quickness; a real student of military conduct. Fort Sill, Oklahoma, was the home of the 4th Army and an artillery unit.

As mentioned, the three primary combat elements are infantry, artillery, and armor (tanks). These units get to wear special ascots: yellow (armor), red (artillery), and blue (infantry). In addition, the infantry wears a blue shoulder cord. Here I was all decked out in my rows of ribbons, including my Army Commendation Medal, Combat Infantry Badge, and blue ascot and shoulder cord. The lieutenant was in the Signal Corps, and he had relatively little to show with ribbons or unit patches. I was wearing two patches, 9th Infantry and 4th Army. My guess is that the lieutenant's commanding officer probably had fewer decorations, ribbons, and patches than I was wearing, so this young "shavetail[7]" was somewhat awestruck by this sergeant who was inspecting his troops.

I finished the inspection and reported to the lieutenant. I also reported the name of the supernumerary, the top soldier in the group who is not assigned but is the replacement if needed. This surprised the young lieutenant. He had forgotten about a supernumerary. Wow—this officer was learning a lot. This was probably his first guard duty detail since he had become an officer—a ninety-day wonder out of OCS (officer candidate school). They must not do much guard duty in the Signal Corps.

It was time to march the men to the command post and post the guards. The lieutenant had a jeep; I was to march the men the quarter mile as he followed. As we were marching, I saw a little jog in the road and thought to myself, *Okay, Weitzel; you want to show your stuff to this ninety-day wonder? How about a little smart marching maneuver?* Again, Captain Risor was big on smartness, precision, and a sharp looking and performing unit or company. He liked to do little maneuvers that

7 Shavetail: The U.S. Army second lieutenants are called shavetails because they are often untrained and untested, like the young mules and horses in the old cavalry, whose tails were customarily shaven as a warning to handlers and riders.

demonstrated that his unit was a cut above the rest. I had great respect for the good captain.

As we marched, I called out the cadence to some old infantry march. I told the squad that we were going to impress the young lieutenant by doing a special maneuver called the oblique right[8] and that I hoped that they remembered it from basic training. "Don't let me down, guys. This will put us in good for the night." We got to the jog in the road and instead of the normal routine I smartly called out, "Squad, oblique right, march!"

They performed it flawlessly. An oblique right is seen often in military marching maneuvers on parade grounds or by marching bands at football halftime shows. It is where an entire group marching in one direction turns 45, 90, or 180 degrees. It takes precision. Everyone has to be alert, sharp, and smart in the execution. If done well, it is impressive. What a show! The troops performed perfectly. I had the won over the squad's heart, mind, and will. They were taking a liking to this military performance by this hardened sergeant.

The rest of the night turned out to be a breeze. The lieutenant got a military education. This guard duty detail was two hours on and two hours off. I did the shift changes every two hours while the lieutenant stayed at the command post.

Most of the time, between changes, the officer and the sergeant of the guard sat and talked, but I did not. I knew that the lieutenant wanted to ask me about my time in Vietnam, but I was not inclined to discuss it. I just lay on a bunk and rested. I think that frustrated the lieutenant, who wanted to be the one in charge, but this buck sergeant had taken command of the squad and duty detail.

There are several types of power—personal, position, knowledge, and delegation. I had most if not all of them, and the lowly lieutenant was learning another valuable leadership lesson: position and title do not necessarily mean power. Early in the morning, we were called to report to the provost marshal's office to pick up one of our own who had been

---

8 The command "Right oblique, march" is given while marching at quick time. The command of execution will be marching to the right oblique from line, given as the right foot strikes the ground, as this involves a movement to the right. At the command of execution, your next step would be one more thirty-inch step to the front with your left foot. Your next step would be to face 45 degrees to the right by pivoting on the ball of the left foot and, at the same time, take a thirty-inch step in the oblique with your right foot. During the execution of this movement, the arms continue their swing but are not allowed to swing wide from the body. Continue to march in the right oblique until given another command.

drunk and disorderly. The lieutenant asked me to take his jeep and pick up the offending party, so I took the driver and a big private with me. When we walked into the office, the place quieted down. It was Friday night, and several GIs had been picked up by the MPs. They turned to look at this buck sergeant all decked out with ribbons, patches, and insignia. I got the sense that at this headquarters battalion they did not see very many decorated soldiers. After all, headquarters personnel are paper pushers, not the mud-and-blood bunch.

The drunken private was in sorry shape. He would be feeling it later on, and when his CO would call him up on charges Monday morning and give him a drop in rank and pay grade. We dropped the private off at his company and returned to the command post. As I gave the lieutenant the charge papers, he gave me a rather quizzical look. I could tell he was unsure what he was to do with them, and I did not want to make him feel totally inept, so I gently reminded him that he needed to complete the necessary forms. I thought to myself, *Don't they teach you ninety-day wonders anything in OCS?* First light came, and the lieutenant released the men from duty. As I walked back to my room, I wondered what the young lieutenant would be telling his friends in the BOQ (bachelor officers' quarters).

On Monday morning, when I reported to work, the chief walked by my desk and said, "Sergeant Wetzel (he called me Wetzel), it seems you made quite an impression on some people during your guard duty detail. Congratulations." And he walked away. Word spread. The old chief looked good, and I guess the squad and the lieutenant had been somewhat impressed.

That's us, "The Old Reliables."

Right, Lieutenant Joseph Zukin, Jr.?

EASY BIVOUAC

A few weeks before my end of service, the battalion was assigned to a field exercise, which entailed the whole battalion going out in the field for two weeks. Since I was just temporarily assigned (a hundred days) to headquarters battalion, I did not have any field gear, and that was fine with me.

The chief asked me if I would like to join the section in the field exercise, and I politely told him that that would not be my first choice. He expected that answer and told me I could stay behind, but I would have to lay low and fend for myself for chow.

"No problem, chief. We jungle warriors know how to fend for ourselves. Don't worry; I'll find an open mess hall."

He gave me half of a smile, and for the next couple of weeks I read to my heart's content, went to movies, and just relaxed. What are you going to do with an old warrior, take away his CIB?

THE RIDE HOME

Mom and Dad were excited that I was coming home for good. They had written that they wanted to drive to Oklahoma to pick me up. On the morning of my discharge, they were in their red Cadillac out in front of battalion headquarters, waiting for me. The sight of them has become one of my fondest recollections. I wonder what the old chief, young lieutenant, and waiting clerks were thinking. Probably they were saying to themselves, "There goes one of God's Lunatics!"

TALLY-HO GREEN!

EPILOG

As the curtain rises on the current chapter of my life, family, friends, and my brother have peppered me with questions. It is only now, after some years, that I am able to open this Pandora's Box and release the 10,000 evils that have been repressed for so long. Upon returning from Vietnam, even during that cab ride home, I worked hard at suppressing the images, experiences, and thoughts of Hell's Backyard. I had no desire to hold on to anything that had happened during those thirteen months. My goal was to get back to a normal life, be with family, and enjoy working again at Frontier Village Amusement Park. Wow, what a contrast! From fun, merriment, and laughter to mud, blood, and exhaustion, and then hopefully back to the Valley Of The Heart's Delight.

Special folks have asked me how long it took me to unwind and not to feel that I had to fight my combat reactions. Each combatant's adjustment time is different. I suspect that some guys never fully got back to a civilized balance of dealing with anger and relationship challenges. Thinking back, the first year or so after my discharge was most challenging, as I consciously fought the urge to react with violence and survival skills. Man is conditioned by "fight-or-flight" response, but combat infantrymen are trained to fight. The military does a marvelous job of brainwashing the flight (or escape) instinct out of a soldier and making an overpowering urge to fight the dominant instinct. As Joe Zukin has so often said, "It is the primeval drive to kill or be killed; it is that simple and raw. It is like a mother's unflinching drive to do whatever is necessary to protect her innocent young." The military's biggest injustice was that it failed to have a program to acclimate the returning combat warrior to a peaceful condition. Oh, maybe the soft duty at Fort Sill was the military's way of helping me to unwind, but I received no special guidance or support in dealing with the adjustment from hostile survival tactics to acceptable civilian behavior.

I find that on occasion, when conditions are just so, my combatant's instinct rears its fiery head, and I have the urge to take swift and decisive action in dealing with a challenging or hostile situation. One must understand that combat infantrymen are trained and conditioned—mental-

136

ly, physically, and psychologically—to come out on top of any situation, bar none. They do not hesitate, think, or pause. It is all conditioned re-action—immediate, swift, and overpowering. Anything less may mean certain death. Combat is a zero-sum game. It is kill or be killed! It is your life or your death. It is the lion against the Christian, and sometimes you are not sure which one you are. This is raw, brutal, and in-your-face survival. The enemy has a gun, bayonet, explosives, and in many cases much more, and his supreme objective is to kill you before you kill him. One's entire body, mind, and spirit are wound up to kill the enemy and to keep living. There is no thought, no remorse, no concern—only a condi-tioned reaction. The combat soldier is a ticking bomb, ready to explode at any triggered moment, and there were many such moments. The train-ing and conditioning are such that the mind, body, and spirit act as one to advance, attack, and kill. There is no half-hearted attempt, no second chance. It is a winner-takes-all game, and the combat soldier gets only one shot if he is lucky. The military motto is: "The quick or the dead!" That is the bottom line. The act of suppressing such a deep-rooted in-stinct is not a simple or easy process. The killing fire burns hot and deep in the combat soldier, and those embers smolder for a very long time.

I tried to suppress not only these conditioned reactions, but also thoughts, images, and memories. Upon returning home, I wanted the sanity and calmness of a civilian life. I hung up my uniform, far back in the closet, and shoved my medals, ribbons, and insignia into a Ziploc bag and buried them in the back of a desk drawer. I was trying to hide those horrific thirteen months. For decades, those reminders were hid-den away. I told my brother that I even hid away my well-earned Army Commendation Medal certificate, and to this day, I cannot remember where I buried it. Someday my son or nephews will come across it when they are cleaning out my worldly possessions, and I hope that they will do me the honor of framing and displaying it in my memory. When I took off my uniform for the last time at Fort Sill, I never again wore it. One of my big regrets is that I never had a picture (or portrait) of me taken in my dress uniform with all my ribbons on display. Another regret is that I never shared the military part of my life with my Mom (Bea), Dad (Paul), or my late wife (Debbie). Thankfully, my brother (Allen), sister-in-law (Susan), nephews (Sean and Tod), son and daughter-in-law (Tim and Jennifer), and granddaughter (Samantha) will know of some of my lifetime experiences.

An important discipline in warfare is to never travel down the same trail twice, whether patrolling an area or returning from a night ambush. If Charlie knew that GIs were in the area, he would set up an ambush or booby traps along the trail in hopes that the lazy GI would come along again and wham! While at Fort Sill, Oklahoma, I received a letter from someone in the platoon who told me that the VC had ambushed his squad that had been returning from a night patrol on the same trail on which they had gone out. Wham! Seven injured and two dead. That was a cardinal sin! Charlie knew that the American GI would take the easy route, and that was the GIs one inherent weakness—laziness.

As a fighting unit, First Platoon, Charlie Company, 4th Battalion performed with honor, distinction, and valor. We were recognized for our contributions and sacrifices. We lost some valiant soldiers, kicked some serious ass, and completed our many missions. We were a tight unit, but after the war we drifted our separate ways. I am just as guilty as any of us for not keeping up contacts and relationships. Mail goes both ways. Now, decades later, a few loyal and dedicated fellas have formed a reunion group that meets every other year. I have been invited several times, but for some inexplicable reason I cannot move myself to join them. One side of me desperately wants to be reunited and to share the camaraderie of times past, but another part of me does not want to go any deeper into those memories, those black, cavernous crevices of death, destruction, and hellfire. I am afraid of what I might uncover. (Is Indian Joe of Tom Sawyer fame just around the corner in the dark cave?) It is an uncomfortable choice I face.

As I was writing these stories, they flowed with such ease. I was amazed at how quickly the images came rushing back, and I was seeing my military experiences like watching a two-hour movie. Allen asked me if I had taken any literary license in my musings. For a moment, I was offended by his question, but then I realized that for the innocent reader I had written things foreign, strange, and out of the ordinary. It must be hard for the vast portion of the population to relate to the raw realities of military service and hell-bent war. Allen was correct; the reader needs to know. No, there was no need to embellish with literary license the antics, trials, or tribulations of the bizarre events. As Joe Zukin said, "Some guys just cannot cope with the rigors of training." Allen, realizing that my "turning-in-my-gear" story was so much out of character for me language-wise, asked if I had embellished it to enhance readability. "No need to," was my response. In the case of the dirty rifle, worn gear, and hostile response, remember that as combat infantrymen we were at hair-trigger readiness. Our training, conditioning, and actions had sharpened us to present immediate and dominating superiority. Quickness was a survival instinct. We had been trained and conditioned to make things happen! Whatever it took, our situation demanded that we move, move fast, take control, and come out on top. This was a military necessity, and sometimes, as the young private and lieutenant discovered, a curse. Do not challenge the crazy sarge! He's not going to be intimidated by rank or position. No, nothing has been embellished. The event, words, and situation were just as clear and crisp as they had happened forty years ago. I was in a survival situation. I had come out of the jungle after living in it for a year, and I was not about to go back into it. I was going home, and no private or pale-looking lieutenant was going to delay my mission. When that young private presented me with a contradictory situation, my training and conditioning instinctively triggered the upper-hand reaction, and being challenged meant I was going to take a lightning reaction to ensure that I came out on top, bar none!

Allen asked me, too, about my thoughts on the exercise of writing these stories. In some ways, it has been a catharsis, especially in recalling the happier and lighter moments. As I worked on this in the quiet early morning hours, the memories and experiences flowed back, sometimes with great ease. One thought would trigger another, and I could not write them down fast enough. Other times, a single recollection would lead me down a thick jungle thought-path that I had all but forgotten and wished I could. There, suddenly, naked realities would pop up, and forty-plus years of repressed memories would flare up. Damn you, Allen!

Those horrid experiences would ride on my shoulder for days at a time, and then when I had finally forgotten them again in life's daily routines, wham, they'd come back bolder, sharper, and just as real in a sweaty nightmare. Double damn! Those are the stories and experiences that you, the reader, will never know about.

As I have mentioned, it is Allen, my beloved brother, who is so deeply interested in the details and responses of my Vietnam experiences. A close friend of his, Dave Kline, was a 2nd lieutenant with the infantry in Vietnam, but Dave died of cancer at an early age due to Agent Orange, and his death deeply affected Allen. I do not know this for a fact, but I think that Allen secretly longed to fight in that war, but time and circumstances kept him from doing so. He is truly a warrior at heart!

As we sat around his kitchen table talking about the various stories, Allen asked me specific details. His questions were pointed and sharp; they were certainly not expressions of doubt; they simply came from his insatiable curiosity and desire to know all the gritty and intimate details.

Another one of Allen's questions had to do with the number of ribbons I wore. Did I really have three rows on my chest, and was that an exaggeration over what the lieutenant at Fort Sill was wearing? Again, there is no need to embellish the situation or story. People who serve in combat or overseas environments receive many more forms of recognition than do those in stateside service. The Combat Infantry Badge is in itself one of the highest forms of honor for a military person. It shows that one has paid his combat dues. Combat service personnel get to wear their combat unit patch on the right shoulder; their regular unit patch goes on the left. The Ninth Division had several unit and presidential citations, and as an infantry unit, we had blue cords, ascot, and the French fourragères earned by the 9th while serving in France in World War II. I had three ribbons (one row) of Vietnam combat ribbons in addition to my personal recognitions, such as the Army Commendation, Good Conduct, and National Defense. No, the three rows of ribbons were not an overstatement. The lowly lieutenant was fresh out of officer candidate school and had yet to earn his recognition. Yes, he may have had shiny gold, 2nd lieutenant bars on his collar and a Signal Corps insignia, but he lacked the military history recognition of a two-year combat soldier who had just come back from a hostile, overseas war zone. I was loaded down with ribbons, insignia, honors, and recognition. In this situation, rank was not superior to experience. The young lieutenant, on his first guard duty assignment, was up against a more seasoned and experienced leader; my decorated uniform trumped his, and he knew it!

Friends have been impressed with my different military baseball-type caps with the various unit and campaign insignia and medals. Some are unit medals, others are marks of individual recognition, and some are general military service commemorative medals, but all are legitimate and proudly worn.

As for the oblique right marching maneuver, the reader might wonder if I had set that up in advance with the squad. The answer is no. When combat leaders (including sergeants) see an advantageous military situation, we are trained and conditioned to take it. When I saw the jog in the road, the normal response would have been to perform a basic turn, but again I was intent on maintaining the upper hand. I quickly decided to do it one better. I didn't know those soldiers, and I was hoping that they had practiced the oblique right maneuver in basic training. By their ranks, looks, and ages, I surmised that they were fresh troops. I was taking a calculated risk that they would properly perform the routine, but I had no assurances that they would. I certainly hadn't anticipated the jog in the road, and the safer bet would have been to call out the simple command. If the guys flubbed the oblique right, I would have had egg on my face, and the lieutenant would have instantly had the leadership advantage. But, remember—I was just back from the win-lose jungle, and I was a cocky buck sergeant. I had confidence in my leadership skills and in what I was doing. That is the key attitude in combat leadership. One cannot show fear, and a true leader has to be self-assured; we make things happen. Officers are the brains, but the sergeants are the backbone. We deliver the expected results, and I wasn't untested or unproven in this area.

My editor has suggested I put in a few words how I feel about our involvement in Iraq. Again, the stock answer for anyone serving in the role of protector, police, firemen, military, or guard is not to comment or criticize one's superiors. Those decisions and actions are better left with those who have intimate knowledge of the events and situations at hand. What I do feel strongly about is that every citizen has an obligation to give a couple of years to his or her country in some form of national servitude, whether it be military, National Guard, Peace or AmeriCorps, or the Civilian Conservation Corps. Such service helps our communities and also helps build one's character and pride in this great country.

The reader is probably left with one, last lingering question. You have learned a lot about military life, combat conditions, and the reality of jungle warfare. Some things have not been revealed because of their raw and emotional nature. That is also true of your remaining question. Do you want to know how many people I killed? You will never know that answer. Not only will I—or any combat soldier—not tell, but also it is a question that one should never ask. How many lives does a fireman save? How many arrests does a policeman make? How many garbage cans does a garbage man pick up? When you are doing a job, you do not keep count. We had a job to do, and we were trained to do it. The country had sent us to Vietnam (right or wrong), and it expected us to perform our assigned tasks to the best of our abilities, and we did. The TV and military may have reported daily body counts, but that was not something we focused on individually or as a unit. We performed our job, and one part of that job was to kill the enemy. There was no emotion (generally), no thought, no glory, or satisfaction in it. We were put in a situation that demanded performance, and we performed. The country, politicians, and powers-that-be had to wrestle with the morality, ethics, and necessity of the war. We were just the instruments. For the GI in the jungle, a more-fitting question would be how many of his buddies' lives did he save. Thank you, Lemar Jackson.

(Sgt.) Warren P. Weitzel
Vietnam—1967

FAMILY MILITARY HISTORY

As Allen and his wife Susan researched the Weitzel family history, they found reason to believe that its military traditions have deep roots. There are historical facts that indicate that the family might be related to General Godfrey Weitzel of Civil War fame (Union side). We do not know if Grandpa John served in the military, and Allen and I never asked that question. Our Dad served in World War II in the U.S. Marine Corps and was trained as a sniper. Allen captured some of Dad's stories and antics, and a few have been published in the Marine Corps magazine Leatherneck. Our blood uncle, Warren, (Dad's brother) served in the Third Army in World War II under General George S. Patton. We sadly regret that we have no stories or additional facts related to Uncle Warren's military service in Europe.

Our other uncle, Herb (Dad's sister's husband), was in the Military Police for his career, and his stories, too, are lost forever. This gives me even more reason to capture what I can recall of my battlefield adventures. It is our hope that this manuscript will give future family generations a little insight into the rough-and-tumble exploits of my time in the service, and encourage other veterans to capture their own history. Think of me when you enjoy your M&Ms, see an old Vietnam War movie, or encounter a nasty rogue scorpion.

"TALLY-HO GREEN!"

AND THAT'S THE WAY IT IS

As I penned these words of a lunatic's experiences, I wondered how my family had dealt with my situation in Vietnam. I sat down with my brother, Allen, and asked him to enlighten me on the view from the home front. I started by asking how he thought Mom and Dad would have responded to my book. Here are Allen's recollections of that time:

"Dad served as a Marine during World War II. He was an extrovert on the outside, but a quiet and reserved man inside. He did enjoy people. He could tell a good story, but he was also a good listener. He enjoyed reading newspaper and magazine articles about sports, and he was an occasional book reader. Dad would read a book once and remember it, and never read it again. He probably would have read Tally-Ho Green and said he liked it, but he probably wouldn't have talked much about it or Warren's military experiences.

Mom, on the other hand, would have taken a long time to read it and would have made some nice, polite comments about it, but she too would not have talked much about it. Thoughts and comments were generally private things in the Weitzel household.

The perception was one of limited understanding about the war and its magnitude. It was the first television war, and people sat in front of their TVs, watching the evening news with Walter Cronkite. (His closing line was always, "And that's the way it is.")

The news showed some combat actions and gave the body count of the enemy dead and the number of U.S. troops killed. The news covered the bigger battles, such as Tet, Khe Sahn, or Saigon, but it didn't focus on the daily routine of the combat soldiers slugging it out in the mud, heat, and rain, where 90 percent of the time it was sheer boredom broken by sporadic incidents of intense, in-your-face firefights with an elusive enemy.

To Dad, and people of his generation, the Vietnam War was not a real war like World War II. In the Second World War, there were battle lines, enemy territories to be seized, and a definite objective to be realized: the defeat of Nazi Germany, Imperial Japan, and Italy—Hitler, Tojo, and Mussolini.

144

Vietnam was a little country in Southeast Asia, and we were there to help the country fight off communism. The short news snippets did not fully encompass the scope and magnitude of the events taking place. People could turn off their televisions and radios and ignore the events if they got tired of hearing about them, unlike the daily reminders (rationing of gas, food, clothing, cars) of the Second World War.

Mom and Dad never worried that Warren would not be coming home. They did not know what Warren was experiencing in the teaming jungles and soggy rice paddies. Their vague impression was that Warren's squad would go out in the jungle for a couple of days and come back to camp and rest for a week before going back out again. The idea of an AK-47 round with Warren's name on it never entered their consciousness.

That doesn't mean they did not think about Warren and family friends (Dave Kline, Gerry Wilhite, Pat Hanna, and my high school buddies) who were over there. It just was not a tangible war to which everyone was making some sort of direct sacrifice and contribution.

The letters that Warren sent, scratched on the cardboard top of C-rations boxes, contained maybe a paragraph or two of how Warren was doing, which was always "fine."

Mom and the family were good about daily correspondence, and Mom would regularly ask me if I had written to Warren that day. Mom, having been through this while Dad was overseas in World War II, knew the importance of regular letters from home. Mom was always sending letters and packages to her son and other family friends.

It was my job to make daily runs to the Santa Clara post office to send off a package or two. The postal clerks got to know me quite well and would often jump me to the head of any line. Of course, an occasional gift of a complimentary five-ride ticket book to Frontier Village certainly helped.

Someone would occasionally ask how Warren was doing. It might be a postal or grocery clerk, employee, neighbor, or family friend, but people were cautious and busy with their daily lives. Since Warren's news home was guarded and limited, the standard family response was that he was fine.

I was busy with school and work, and had to squeeze in postal drop-offs and letter writing. I would write a short letter during my lunch breaks and often write about happenings at the beloved Frontier Village. Employees might ask about Warren, but more often it was Joe Zukin, the president of Frontier Village, who would ask me about my brother's situation. I never really knew if Joe's inquiries were from one veteran to another, a genuine inquiry, or an employer anxious to have a valuable employee return safe and sound. In many ways it was probably a mixture of all three.

Mom and Dad would share letters but seldom any deep dialogue about their content. I remember one or two letters from Warren that Mom didn't share with me. She offered some soft excuse that she wanted to reread it or would share it a little later, but she would somehow forget to pass it along.

In hindsight, I believe that the public's opinion of the war was 180 degrees off center. The disjointed news (television) focused only on the sensational aspects. Stories about medics saving lives, the heroics of helicopter pilots, and infantrymen dealing with booby traps were not in the mainstream media.

One got the feeling that death and disfigurement always happened to somebody else and not to friends or family. People just went about doing their jobs; the war was somebody else's problem."

And so, "that's the way it was on the home front."

QUESTIONS AND ANSWERS

As this book was being edited and prepared for print, some friends and fellow workers who read the rough drafts of his book, began to ask specific questions. So as not to disturb the train of thought I had when I was recording my memories and to maintain the continuity of each chapter, I have provided this Q/A section to field last-minute inquiries, with the topics not presented in any specific order.

Q/ What were the sleeping arrangements while out in the jungle?

A/ Falling asleep was easy, as we would be tired from our jungle travel. Usually, one of the two guys at each defensive position would sleep while the other kept watch. After a couple hours, he would wake up his buddy, who would then keep watch. Unfortunately, on several occasions, both guys would be asleep when a sergeant checked on them.

We would lay a poncho on the ground or lean one up against a tree. Usually, the only time we would dig a foxhole was when we set up early in the evening and had the time to "dig in." Most of the time we were on the move, and we would just plop down in a "circle-the-wagons" formation.

Q/ How often did you get mail? Could you send mail?

A/ We seldom got mail while in the jungle. Maybe if we were at an artillery camp for a few days they would fly in a bag of mail with the Huey resupply helicopter, but generally we would get mail only when we got back to base camp (Bearcat), which was seldom. We might have two or three months' worth of mail waiting for us, and I was the mail champion. A special thank you to Mom, Dad, Allen, family, friends, Joe, and others. Mom wrote almost every day. Any mail was a welcome reminder of home. If we had the time, we would write a letter home using the cardboard from C-rations boxes instead of regular paper. We would turn the cardboard inside out to create a clean writing surface, write a short message, and "seal" it with a piece of elephant grass or vine by punching a couple of holes in the end flap with a bayonet and tying it closed. We would write our APO (Army Post Office) return address and write the word "free" in the postage stamp space. When a resupply helicopter arrived, we would drop the letter in a small bag next to the door gunner who would then mail them for us.

147

I have a collection of C-rations letters I mailed home that Mom saved. They are a nice chronicle of my time in Vietnam. As I re-read those letters, I was surprised at the events I wrote about and the ones that I kept to this day. What a history for my grandchildren!

After being at Fort Sill for a couple of months, my backlogged mail from Vietnam began to catch up with me. I remember I had another big load of it arrive after a couple of months. As I got closer to coming home for good, Mom, Dad, and Allen began to tail off on their letters. They had been dutifully faithful for nearly two long, hard years.

Q/ I have heard that there was a lot of drug usage in Vietnam by American soldiers. Is that true?

A/ Well, I cannot speak for the other units (armor, artillery, chopper pilots, or base camp personnel), but I never saw it in our unit. Hell, the guys were always bugging me for my cigarettes (from the C-rations box), since I did not smoke. We would be lucky to get any resupplies for several days at a time, and then it was food and ammo, not much else. We wanted dry socks but seldom got those. No, I never experienced any drug usage in the First Platoon. We forty-two guys were always around each other, and the guys were lucky just to get a regular cigarette let alone some street drugs. In the movie Forrest Gump, you see guys at a base camp with Lieutenant Dan, enjoying a barbecue with beer, sodas, steaks, and rolled toilet paper. Yeah, right! Some units reported that they hunted deer and had venison barbecues. Heck, I never even saw a deer "in country."

We got twelve sheets of toilet paper and four cigarettes in our C-rations box. We never had a barbecue, and maybe once in Bearcat did we have any iced beer or sodas. No—our unit must have been the runt of the group because we were always out in the field and on the move. It was a tough gig.

Q/ How did the officers address you?

A/ As Lieutenant Joe Zukin will tell you, everyone in the army was addressed by his last name. Joe still cannot recall Sergeant Uzoni's—his jeep driver's—first name. A first name in the army is a person's rank: private, sergeant, lieutenant, captain, etc.

Q/ Do you have your ribbons and awards on display?

A/ For many decades I wanted to forget my time and experience in Vietnam. I was proud of my service and received "excellent" evaluations throughout my time, but I just did not want to think about the dark experiences of combat. Therefore, I buried my medals and awards in some hidden drawer and gave away my uniform (Class A) and went on with my life. My brother, Allen, gently prodded me in later life to set down my experiences on paper and dig out my medals for the family to keep as heirlooms. I am glad he nudged me to do so.

A few years ago, I dug out my military records (DD214) and had my medals, awards, and insignia framed and put on display in my home. I still cannot locate my Army Commendation certificate, but the rest of my history is on display. I have several military baseball-type caps I wear now, with the various units, campaign, and commemorative medals. All are legitimate and proudly worn.

Q/ What is "double tapped"?

A/ The military uses many hand signals to direct aircraft on a carrier deck, fire artillery shells, or direct infantrymen in a combat encounter. Remember, combat infantrymen are engaged with the enemy. They kill the enemy or will be killed. This is not some childhood game of cowboys and indians. It is mortal combat, raw, brutal, and wicked. Combat infantrymen are trained to survive, to come out on top in any hostile situation. Our job was to kill! Sorry, that's what we did—kill! If VC, whether adults, children, men, women, young or old, were threatening in any way, we would kill them. Even in Saigon, young children would ride by on a bicycle and toss a hand grenade into an open truck or jeep to kill Americans. We know about the human bombers in Baghdad. The "double tapped" signal meant to shoot the bastard! It was not a verbal command or order, just a couple open-palm fingertip taps to one's helmet (steel pot), and the prisoner/VC was "wasted." "No sir, no one gave an order to shoot anyone." (Just a silent, untraceable signal that came from somewhere.)

Q/ Did you ever have a firefight where you needed or got air support? What kind was it? Hueys, Spookys, or Phantoms?

A/ I do not recall ever having air support called in for some direct action for our involvement. We were light recon and ranger (sniff and spook) engagements. Once or twice at a firebase (light duty) we took harassing fire during the night, and the base called in a couple of Hueys (UH-1D) to spray the perimeter with M-60 and Gatling gun fire, and that sent Charlie scurrying off. However, no, nothing where we were up against a superior force. As previously mentioned, our contact was pretty much nose-to-nose with the VC (a few feet or meters apart), so we didn't have the distance necessary for safe air support. We preferred "duck-and-dodge" maneuvers. Our whole training had been to stand alone and fight. That one time when I led those ten great guys on the 9,000-meter night patrol without air or artillery support really drove home the importance of our individual performance. I saw a Cobra gunship in action once, from a distance, and twice saw a jet drop napalm on a VC village base camp. That was impressive. And scary.

Q/ Did you have trouble with your M-16 jamming?

A/ The issue of the M-16 jamming was a cause for concern, as one could imagine. The predecessor to the M-16 was the AR-15 (automatic rifle), used by the marines in Vietnam. With this early model, they encountered serious jamming problems that in several instances caused needless deaths in heated battles. Our division was one of the first (if not the first) to get the M-16 and use it in training, so we were a test group. During our training we kept it clean, but it did tend to jam without lubrication. The rounds would get lodged in the chamber due to bits of dirt and debris. The use of light oil helped minimize the jamming, but we quickly discovered that in the heat and dampness of the jungle the oil was quickly washed away. We needed a more permanent solution.

In jungle warfare, one does not have the time or conditions for a thorough rifle cleaning. When we would take a quick rest break during our jungle travel, the guys would use a towel (from around one's neck) or an old tee shirt to wipe out the chamber or run a swab down the barrel. We were always begging or stealing cleaning rods from each other. They were hard to come by, and whenever the supply sergeant at base camp would send a load of them to us in the field, they would quickly be snatched up. During longer breaks, we would empty our twenty-round ammunition clips and wipe off each bullet before reloading the magazine.

Dirty rounds were the biggest jamming culprits. The dirt and grime on a round would cause it to jam in the rifle's chamber. When we could get them, we would load a hot-tipped tracer round every fifth bullet. These were a big help in night firefights. Wish I had had them when I came up against that big banana leaf. Tracer rounds are damn hot, and one can feel their heat as they zing by the ear.

The M-16 was a durable weapon except when it jammed. It was easy to take apart, wipe down, clean, and reassemble. Unlike the bulkier M-14, the M-16 was made for jungle warfare. We depended upon our weapon to keep us alive, so we seldom had to tell anyone to clean his weapon. Although we never had formal inspections out in the jungle, we would periodically check weapons. The guys were very good about using any slack time to clean their M-16s.

From the time we received our M-16 in basic training until we left Vietnam, some twenty months later, that weapon was with us all the time! We slept with it, went to the bathroom with it, ate, marched, and made love with it. It was fired every day. We used blank ammunition during basic and live rounds during advanced individual training. In Vietnam, out in the jungle, we would fire our weapon at least once in the morning and once in the evening. We wanted to ensure that no rounds would be jamming in the chamber. If we were in a no-fire zone, the lieutenant would tell us when we could fire. If it were a free-fire zone, then the guys would shoot off a couple of rounds into the air. We needed to check our weapons, but we were also mindful not to waste ammunition. We had too many narrow escapes where we ran low on ammo.

Although it was not recommended that we keep a round chambered, we all did so. It often meant the difference between living and dying. Thank you, Lemar Jackson. Once we started using 90-weight tank oil as a lubricant, our jamming problems were greatly reduced. A round might jam if it had not been properly positioned in the clip, but even with dirty rounds, the oil helped slide a cockeyed round smoothly into the chamber. My M-16 never let me down in a critical situation or firefight, thank God!

Q/ You participated in track and cross-country in high school sports. Did that conditioning help you excel over and above the average recruit?

A/ Yes. I think being physically fit and all that walking I did at Frontier Village as a park manager were probably a plus. Most of the guys in basic were in good shape; I don't remember any real heavy or fat guys. Of course, the daily physical training, diet, and running worked miracles. It was more stamina and endurance than it was physical. Could one keep going sixteen hours? The guys who smoked had it tougher. They would want a smoke break, but we would keep marching, running, or "engaging the enemy" during a long training exercise. It was all about mental, physical, and emotional stamina. Bearing up under the pressures of the endless training was the real challenge. (When was it ever going to end?) Seven long, grueling months. "Come on, Coach, put me in the game!"

Q/ What about timepieces? Did someone have a watch or time-piece to make sure that you had a way to reference time on patrols where you had to be at a set location at a precise time? Also, if the "guard duty watch" was set at two hours in between members of the squad, how did you keep track of that arrangement? If you did have a timepiece, how did it survive the rigors of the climate?

A/ Watches? What watches? No, we were not issued watches. Some guys had them. I either broke or lost my personal watch during AIT. Platoon sergeants and lieutenant had them. Most of the time we just traveled until we reached our destination. When we did that 9,000-meter jaunt, a couple of guys had watches, so they kept me informed. At night, when doing guard duty in the jungle, we would just watch the moon and stars (lots of stars), and wake up our buddy when we got tired. On the other hand, if he had the watch, we would share it. "Soldier, if the army wanted you to have a watch, they would have issued one to you!"

Q/ Your story seems to be a little condescending toward the support units and the roles they played. Why are you so down on the rear echelon?

A/ I guess you're right. I've been told by a couple of people that I didn't seem to respect the various support units, cadre, or officers. Some have pointed out that I was unduly hard on the young private accepting my rifle and the privates at the helicopter pad and personnel section, and almost disrespectful of the shavetail lieutenant during guard duty. Yes, I guess I was.

Let me see if I can put this into a better perspective for the reader. This may be difficult for anyone other than a combatant to understand, but here goes. War is intense. It is immediate, direct, and deadly. Infantry combatants are trained to locate, close with, engage, and kill the enemy! No ambiguity. No questions. No hesitation—just split-second action. This is hard to understand. I think that is why it was so difficult for returning veterans to adjust to the soft and laid-back homeland style of life. Infantrymen have just one guiding survival instinct: be quick or dead! That is drummed into us from day one and all through the seven months of in-your-face training. Move, move now, be decisive, and come out on top!

That's how the 9th Division (Charlie Company, 4th Battalion, 39th Infantry) was trained. We had a hotly intense mission before us in the jungles of Vietnam. We faced a fiercely competitive enemy, one who was willing to die for his homeland, and his tactics and environment were hostile. We were going to be small units (ten guys), oftentimes detached from the platoon, on our own for long periods of time. We had to rely on our hair-trigger responses. (Those VC and booby traps are killers!)

Unfortunately, like Captain Risor with Major Smith and Colonel Bell, if things don't go the way we plan, we'll take aggressive action to get the intended results, bar none! Battle-tested combat infantrymen are action-oriented, and nothing, nothing slows us down or deflects our attention from the intended mission, whether that be combat engagement, getting to a destination, or turning in a pitted and worn rifle.

The reader needs to understand what drives a combat soldier: survival. Hard and fast survival. Orders are not questioned. Action is taken. Missions are accomplished. And, the enemy is killed, without thought and with dispatch. The highest calling in the army is that of a combat-hardened infantryman. He's the whole reason that other personnel and units exist: to support him! His call to duty is the highest, and he experiences and endures the lowest forms of privation.

He is cocky, arrogant, disciplined, and fast. He has paid his combat dues, and he proudly wears the Combat Infantry Badge at the top of his chest of campaign and military ribbons. Only the Medal of Honor has a higher status.

If the infantryman is an NCO (noncommissioned officer), or officer, then you know he makes things happen. He has the guts and gumption to get things done. He will not make or accept excuses. Performance counts. Without it, he and his men are dead!

So, we're sorry if we weren't kinder and gentler to the support units and personnel. Yes, we understand the important roles they play in our survival and mission accomplishments. Unfortunately, we infantrymen do not have time for high-fives, pats on the back, or leisurely performance. Our survival may depend on that twenty-round M-16 clip being emptied in five seconds and getting things accomplished with speed and dispatch, not taking eight hours to type up twenty-five assignment orders.

Yep, as Jim Haines reminded me, "Warren, it's eleven guys in support of the one combat (infantry, armor, artillery) soldier in the field. We fight anytime of the day or night. Ours is not an eight-hour day. We demand that the support troops jump when we bark!" Farmer, toss me some ammo!

Under battlefield conditions, men trained for action must make split-second decisions when they are wrapped in the heavy fog of war. When such men at the bayonet tip have been firefighting for so long, they are tired, numb, and sapped of all human courtesies. And so, when the combat infantryman barks, others must jump. These combatants are walking detonators carrying the untold weight of high explosives. They are emotionally charged and quick in action. They have little patience for the delays and excuses of the rear echelon. "Only lunatics can be completely original," Warren P. Weitzel.

Q/ You mentioned that you became the platoon sergeant when Lieutenant Walker joined the first platoon about six months into your tour of duty. When did you first become a sergeant?

A/ A long answer to a short question. From the first week after my induction in April 1966, I was a sergeant. The term of endearment was "acting jack" (don't know why they are called that). We held the position but not the official rank or pay. The military has an excellent chain of command. Somebody is always in line to move up should a leader become unable to command. Unlike some military organizations that do not have a fluid chain of command, the army keeps the pipeline full. Other countries do not follow such a program.

In one of my delightful conversations with Joe Zukin, infantry lieutenant stationed in Germany in World War II, he told me that the life expectancy of a lieutenant in combat was mere minutes. I believe the same was true in Vietnam. Should a lieutenant be killed, the platoon sergeant would take over, then the senior squad (fire team) leader, then corporals, and perhaps the privates, should most of the platoon be wiped out.

When Joe was in basic training at Fort Robinson, he, too, was given the black armband with sergeant's chevrons. One wears those until he messes up, then someone else gets a shot at the position.

If I recall correctly, about the second or third week of basic, we acting jacks had the armbands taken away and were given permanent sergeant stripes to sew onto our fatigues and dress uniforms. I guess we had proven ourselves during those first weeks of adjustment to military life. I never had to wear private, corporal, or specialist insignias. Of course, as we got properly promoted in permanent rank, our pay rate increased. On my DD214 (discharge papers), it says my grade was sergeant (T) at the time of discharge. One cannot be a permanent sergeant without at least three years of military service. The T is a temporary rank designation.

Q/ I never heard that story about you challenging your new company captain. Tell us that story.

A/ For the life of me, I cannot remember our company commander's name after Captain Risor rotated out to his new assignment. I do recall that Captain Risor had spoiled us, and we did not care for our new commander. Of course, we saw very little of him, but I do remember one incident where he was inspecting our night position after we had had a particularly rough day of heavy traveling. He was coming around to inspect the platoon foxholes and was not happy with what he was seeing. Our positions were not deep enough for his liking, and he wanted us to keep digging them deeper. It must have been well past 9:00 P.M., and the guys were bushed. We just wanted to eat and get some rest. His concern was genuine; he wanted us to have the proper protection should we be attacked, but his method of barking orders to the lowly grunt wasn't being well received. When he got to my foxhole, I was in no mood for some starch-fatigued captain telling the men and me what needed to be done. He was telling us how to provide adequate protection, and he did not even have a camouflaged CIB on his clean uniform blouse. I don't recall my exact words, but something to the tune of, "Sir, with all due respect, these foxholes are at our normal combat depth." The look on his face told me that he was not too pleased with my comment; he told me that they would be dug deeper. "Yes sir," was my reply.

Lieutenant Walker gave me a piercing look as they departed. When Lieutenant Walker returned, he let me know that he understood my frustration but cautioned me about challenging officers, especially over minor situations. "Let it go, Sergeant. Do as you are ordered and keep off his radar." I sensed that the good lieutenant wasn't happy with the captain.

Q/ How well did your training terrain match the conditions you found in Vietnam?

A/ Other than the weather, not too well. Kansas is flat, hot, and dry. Vietnam is wet, full of vegetation, and hot as hell. Our environment training focused on two aspects. One of them was stamina: keeping going, like the Energizer Bunny, for sixteen hours a day with fully loaded (seventy-plus pound) packs. We hauled those loads through heavy vegetation, waist-deep mud, chest-high water, and 112-degree heat with 100 percent humidity.

The other focus of our training was tactics, small-unit tactics. Ours was a new type of combat situation. We would often be small units (fire teams) fighting an elusive enemy during brief but intense firefights.

As a platoon or squad, we'd often be a self-contained unit out of artillery or resupply range (triple-canopy jungle) for days at a time. We had to know how to locate, close with, engage, and then kill the enemy.

I would have liked to have received some training in dealing with fire ants, scorpions, leeches, and snakes. Instead, in Kansas it was chiggers and ticks. The 9th Division was an early arrival in terms of the length of the war. We got there in January 1967, and it didn't end until 1974. In many ways, we had to rewrite the combat tactics book for this new type of warfare, Ranger style. As mentioned, the M-16 training went out the window. The dry-fire weapon needed heavy (90-weight oil) lubrication.

Even Lieutenant Walker, West Point, was smart enough to realize his formal training was useless in this hostile environment and new warfare engagement.

Q/ In your combat experience, how was your interaction with members of your squad or platoon and the officers above you? (Joseph Zukin, Jr. 2nd lieutenant infantry, Germany, World War II).

A/ I never had any real difficulties with leadership of my men or the officers. As I have said in the book, I had the greatest respect for the officers, including Captain Risor, Lieutenant Leslie, Lieutenant Walker, and others. Staff Sergeant Tisdel was a great platoon sergeant, and I respected him.

I was a little bit older than most of the guys in the platoon, being twenty-two when drafted. (I think Captain Risor was twenty-nine at the time.) Having worked with Joe, Ed, Keith, and others at Frontier Village had given me a leg up in managing people. I was comfortable being in charge of people; I have a director-type personality. Oh, sure the guys in the squad were testing me those first few weeks of basic training, but I was used to the employees at Frontier Village and their boundary-pushing antics, so I was able to keep my fire team in line. Thankfully, no one ever physically threatened me. Call me names? You bet, but no hostile threats.

I do recall Joe telling me of his early basic-training experiences where one of the soldiers got in his face when he was first made an acting jack. "So why did they make you in charge?" was the belligerent soldier's question. Joe appropriately responded, "They picked me because they believe that I can do the job, and I don't want you to ever challenge me in that way again!" The soldier got the message. Joe held the leadership position, and that was the way it was going to be. If one stands up to the first challenge and meets it head on with resolute firmness, that's usually the end of such difficulties. The word spreads and guys quickly fall into line. Parents call it tough love; sergeants and officers call it brass balls.

Most of us quickly decided whether we wanted to lead or follow. I knew going in that I wanted to be in charge of my own destiny (survival). I do not know if the guys liked me (you will have to ask Corporal James Farmer), but I think they respected what I was trying to do for them and me.

Continuing with Joe's question about interaction in a combat situation: it was certainly a much different situation than during training. We always addressed the officers by rank and name, but we would never salute when out in the field. Nobody wanted the VC having an easy way to identify the officers. Although the units were disciplined, orders and instructions were handled in a much more informal style. Certainly, the chain of command was followed and execution was punctual. With forty guys bonded together elbow to elbow for 365 days in horrible living conditions, a tightness developed. Soldiers could sense what needed to be accomplished, and they did not have to wait for orders. It is almost like the minds of the officer and soldiers became one. We all had a mission: fight the war, protect the officers, and hopefully all come home alive. Most of us kept our personal lives private. Emotional attachment was something nobody wanted. It was generally a military-based type of relationship.

Captain Risor and Lieutenants Leslie and Walker treated us well; they looked out for our well-being. They needed our combat abilities, and we needed their leadership training and expertise. We were one cohesive and crack unit. "Give it to Charlie Company; they'll get it done!"

Q/ How many bullets did you fire off during your time in training and combat?

A/ My best estimate would be between 5,000 and 6,000 rounds, but I have no exact accounting. No wonder my M-16 barrel was so badly pitted.

Q/ How would you describe the feeling of combat?

A/ The rush of combat is as intense as the feeling of being locked in a small, pitch-black room with a deadly, poisonous snake.

MENTORS

Americans are drawn to military leaders, and one could make the case that fighting men are consistently successful in life. I believe that is because they have learned how things really work from the bottom up, and they have seen firsthand the realities of human nature. Three military men, all credits to themselves and their military service, have influenced my life:

My Dad, Corporal Paul W. Weitzel, served in World War II as a marine sniper. Although he did not charge into battle, he trained many a marine in the fine art of marksmanship and in so doing greatly aided the war effort in the Pacific.

Joseph Zukin, Jr., was my mentor at Frontier Village Amusement Park (San Jose, California), and he served as a 2nd lieutenant in Germany just after World War II. He also served in the 9th Infantry Division, 39th Brigade.

Colonel Robert Work is a lifelong family friend. After graduating from San Jose State in the late 1930s, he became a colonel in the US air force, where he had a distinguished career in intelligence.

I salute each of them for their military, life successes, and achievements.

Three other officers deserve recognition for their strong influence upon my humble military service. Captain Risor, Lieutenant Leslie, and Lieutenant Walker were each role models to me as a young soldier in the 9th Division. I admired their professionalism and strong sense of duty. They are a credit to themselves and the U.S. Army. Each of these six military mentors knew the realities of life and the raw realities of war. They know how to mold and build men of character and truly are leaders in their own right. Gentlemen, I salute you!

DIFFICULT JUNGLE TRAIL

What started out as a simple fulfillment of a family member's request has turned out to be a challenging journey down one of life's jungle paths.

It all began when my loving brother, Allen, suggested I commit to paper a few of my military (war) stories. We did not have any written history from our father (Paul), Uncle (Warren), or friend (Colonel Robert Work) of their wartime experiences. Allen felt I owed to future generations to capture my wartime adventures of fighting in the jungles of Vietnam. I had never shared with anyone my trials, tribulations, or horrors of wartime lunacy. God knows, Allen tried to engage me in opening up, but I had locked those events away in my self-imposed bamboo cage. I had no desire to travel down those frightening trails again.

After much gentle prodding, I reluctantly agreed to commit a few of the lighter ones to paper. What started out as a handful of simple tales soon mushroomed into the makings of a wartime chronicle. I would share one or two stories with Allen and friends, and they would pester me for more. Soon those simple stories demanded greater descriptions. The simple, mundane routines of daily jungle survival turned into full chapters of daily hardships, scary experiences, and high-intensity firefights against a persistent enemy.

After a few weeks of writing, I had the makings of a wartime classic. People began urging me to publish my experiences. Allen strongly believed others outside our circle of family and friends might crave the nuts-and-bolts experiences of a shake 'n bake buck sergeant's daily life in the steaming jungle and mud swamps of Vietnam. It seemed the readers wanted to travel shoulder to shoulder with me (in book form) through Hell's Backyard. My war diary was no longer to remain hidden under the jungle's triple canopy.

The writing exercise was a catharsis, and many of the experiences came rushing back with intensity and clarity. The forty years of suppression were like a compressed spring. I was reliving the good, the bad, and the ugly—like it or not. Soon I was hearing from people outside my daily circle of contacts. Outsiders were asking for copies of my draft, so with some great help from my writer brother, Allen and I took the next step in the book-publishing journey.

Writing the initial draft was the easiest part. The words and experiences flowed so fast at times that I could not record them quickly enough on my trusty old typewriter. As I got the drafts completed, Tod Weitzel, nephew, and Ted Kopulos helped with the computerization.

Next, the book was polished for review. It is not just a matter of having an interesting story to tell; a polished presentation and tightly edited package are critical for grabbing a publisher's attention. Today's publishers do not want sloppy material. A writer has only a small window of opportunity to capture a publisher's attention and interest.

Susan Weitzel, my sister-in-law, her brother Ted Kopulos, and my brother Allen each set about to work their magic to correct my many grammatical, typing, spelling, and punctuation errors. Sue read the story from a critical-eye perspective and offered a host of literary suggestions to bring me closer to my intended audience. We did not change the content or embellish any stories but added clarity, perspective, and insight to the daily grind of in-the-trenches wartime life.

My editors have been demanding. They pushed me back to the typewriter for additional pages of text, expanded points, and vivid details. I was told I had to get closer to my readers. Hell, much closer and they would feel the bullets zinging by their ears. "That's what we want," said my thoughtful critics.

The rewrites requested by Allen, Sue, Ted, and Tod were the most challenging part of the project. It was like being back in school again, and the English composition teacher was giving the assignment back to the student and saying; "This is not your best effort; redo it again!" I felt I had done a wonderful piece of storytelling for people to enjoy, but my critics are raising the bar. "Come on, Coach; give me a break here." Oops, a mixed metaphor. My editors are not going to like that.

The project grinds on. It is slow, tedious work, and the end seems to slip further and further away. At times the enthusiasm wanes, but my editors keep me motivated and on point.

I have no illusions about reaching publication. I still have a long row to hoe. Many people have told me that manuscripts and movie scripts oftentimes never see the light of publication or projection. Even if that does not happen, I have at least captured my combat experiences for future family generations.

I can dream of a movie deal or the talk-show circuit, but this is no *Gone With The Wind*. Just experiencing the fringes of the publishing world has made me glad I decided to stay in the amusement field. Writing for a living is too damn challenging. I do not know how my writer brother Allen does it.

"TALLY-HO GREEN!"

YEARS LATER

While fighting in the jungles of Vietnam, and years later, I felt that our unit, Charlie Company, 4/39th Infantry spent nearly all of its time in the field—mud, swamps, jungle, etc.—battling the elements and the Viet Cong. It was my perception that we did not get back to Bearcat base camp very much, and when we did it was only to clean up and re-supply before heading back into battle.

As the years rolled by, I talked with other combat soldiers from our battalion (4th) and saw movies in which soldiers were having extended breaks and barbecues. I wondered if I had just missed the fun or winked out during those times. Charlie Company never had a barbecue that I can remember; perhaps there were one or two times when beer and sodas were made available on a company level. To me it seemed that we just kept humping through the jungle.

I mentioned this perception to my brother, Allen, and he suggested that I try to uncover the facts. He said that knowing such information would help to strengthen my story and perhaps tie up some loose ends.

Thanks to a comrade, Jim Haines, in B Company, I re-established contact with my former commanding officer, Captain Robert Risor. The good captain is now a retired major living in Arkansas, and we have talked and exchanged correspondence a few times. He is a grand gentle-man and a leader with high values and ethics. I have the greatest respect for Major Risor, a tough but fair and respectful leader. He told me once that his goal was to give us the required training so that we would all come home alive.

So, at Allen's persistent urgings, I called the good major and had a nice chat with him on the afternoon of September 17, 2009. He had in-tended to go to a football game at the University of Arkansas, but it was raining. (I thought that a little odd; a good rain never stopped Captain Risor from going forward with our training or combat missions during the monsoons of Vietnam.) Well, after all he has been through, including his helicopter crash in Vietnam, I guess he is entitled to a little comfort at age seventy-three.

So, I asked Major Risor if I was mistaken in my perception of limited rest time back at Bearcat, and he told me, "Warren, you're absolutely right. We had very little rest time; we were out in the field a lot." When we arrived in Vietnam, the plan called for us to become acclimatized before beginning operations, but the battalion commander, Colonel Bell, had us out on patrol operations and road clearings during our first week. While other companies in the battalion had the luxury of adjusting and settling in, Charlie Company was sent out on several select and critical missions.

While we were engaged in basic and advanced training, Colonel Bell told the then–Captain Risor that we were the best company in the battalion (five companies, 900 men). Captain Risor told me that Charlie Company was either the best or the second-best company in the whole brigade (twenty-plus companies, 5,000 men). I learned from the good captain that Colonel Bell, a West Point graduate, expected good results. Charlie Company delivered those results during training and in the jungles of Vietnam. Captain Risor was not out for personal gain. He wanted his men well trained so they could do the job expected and return home safe. Charlie Company was fortunate to have some good companionship and a great bunch of guys who developed into outstanding soldiers.

We were pushed hard in basic and advanced training because everyone knew where we were going and the horrendous conditions we would encounter. The 9th Division was being trained to go into a hotbed of enemy activity, III Corps' area of operation, War Zone C. Colonel Bell wanted his battalion to look good, and he would call on Charlie Company for challenging situations. He would tell Captain Risor what he wanted done, and Captain Risor and Charlie Company would get it done and get it done right. Captain Risor told me that our outstanding ranking during our seven months of intense training was validated when Charlie Company was selected as the honor company to be reviewed by the secretary of the army when he inspected the 9th Division just before our deployment to Vietnam.

Charlie Company excelled in training and mission assignments. While other units had much more rest time, we were given the tougher assignments. Captain Risor did confess to me that at times he pushed us past our boundaries during several critical missions. We were a good group. Captain Risor talked fondly about Staff Sergeant Tisdel, First Platoon's sergeant during training and the first six months in country. Captain Risor always looked out for his men. We were his responsibility and he took that to heart.

Captain Risor told me the story where we had been out on patrol for two to three weeks, a particularly tough mission. When we returned to Bearcat, we had no water for showers. The rear echelon had used up our allotted supply of water. They were clean and refreshed, and Charlie Company returned filthy and smelling like dead rats. Captain Risor was pissed. He said he was so mad that he went to Major Smith, assistant commander, and strongly told him that such treatment was unacceptable. Captain Risor was so heated that Colonel Bell got involved, and Captain Risor demanded that something be done immediately about the situation. The good captain got quick results. An emergency supply of water was ordered up for the troops of Charlie Company.

I always enjoy my conversations with Major Risor, Lieutenant Joe Zukin, Sp. 4 Jim Haines, Corporal James Farmer, and retired Colonel Robert Work. These are great gentlemen, outstanding soldiers, and a wealth of information and enlightenment. Risor, Haines, and Farmer often clarified my occasional hazy recollections and filled in the blanks on things I have blocked out or forgotten. I deeply appreciate Major Risor taking the time to validate my thinking involving our field time. I've always believed, from what I experienced, that we were the vanguard unit for the 4/39th. We were grilled with seven months of intense tactical (Ranger-style) training and faced a hostile enemy and environment. I was just a grunt[9], but I like to consider myself a perceptive person. It was satisfying for me to have Risor verify my impression of very little base camp time and critical-missions activity.

As Allen reminded me, this ties up several loose ends to my wartime family history. Jim Haines recently corrected a fact for my readers and me. I have said several times that there are nine men in support for one combat soldier. Jim said, "Warren, I've always heard it was eleven support for every combat soldier." Wow, that makes us infantry, armor, and artillery guys even more special.

Maybe what Lieutenant Walker told me was true when he said that the company commander had specifically requested Sergeant Weitzel for the critical 9,000 meter LZ security mission. Thank you, Captain Risor!

---

9 Grunt: a name given to the American GIs by the Vietnamese because of the sound the GI makes when he's loading on the seventy pounds of supplies he carries.

NO, SIR!

The other night I had one of those restless and sleepless nights. You know; the kind where something bothersome keeps rattling around in your mind and you cannot get it resolved, so you lie there, tossing and turning.

In my situation, I had three matters about this book and related matters that were playing on me. I had received a phone message from the organizer of the 9th Division Reunion, and he was hoping that I would attend this year's event. Then, my brother Allen, family editor of this book, called to ask that I include a small paragraph or two about my experiences with Agent Orange, the defoliant used in Vietnam. He explained that it had been a hot news topic back in the States while I was in Vietnam.

The most disturbing matter had to do with Allen's query to potential publishers. Oh, the letter was fine—great, in fact. However, now the realization was starting to set in that my story might actually be unveiled to outsiders. I was starting to get cold feet.

It was okay when a few close friends and family read a few of the lighter excerpts, but now strangers would be looking into my soul. What would happen if people actually read the book and started asking probing questions? For over four decades, I had hid my story under a blanket and suppressed my fears. Now I was not so sure that I wanted to let others into my world.

Sure, I'm proud of my military service and excellent record, and I'm proud of the book. I stand behind my story, but I still have lingering and haunting fears. That's one reason I keep making excuses to myself for not attending the 9th Division reunion. I'm afraid of my "Indian Joe" in the dark cave and having him reaching out and grabbing my arm, just like it happened in Huckleberry Finn.

No, sir; I'm not so sure that I'm ready for the story to be published. I am more afraid of those 10,000 mind evils than I was with those bullets whizzing by my ears or kicking dirt up around my feet. I can still hear the snapping sound of AK-47 rounds from the VC on the trail behind Lemar Jackson, and I see the shadows of that banana leaf VC lurking like Indian Joe. All of this is still too real and imminent.

The book has taken on a life of its own. What started out as just a few funny stories for the family has turned into a publishing adventure. The success or failure will rest with Allen's efforts. That's what scares me. He's good, and he'll no doubt turn it into a huge success. I may have given the book its substance, but he's giving it life! Our great publisher, Llumina Press, is giving it character.

Some might say that I'm experiencing post-traumatic stress disorder, but I don't know about that. Bad dreams haunt a lot of people, especially after terrifying events such as car accidents. I'm sure that a policeman who is drawn upon with a knife or gun probably has similar dreams. Sure, close-quarters combat is a little more stressful, perhaps. It's true; a combat soldier is in a constant state of cat and mouse. Unlike a policeman who may have periods when danger is not lurking, an infantryman is always at the constant ready, and that can be wearing. The infantryman's life purpose is to take the life of his enemy. Combat is Darwinism at its highest level, the ultimate position of power.

The survival game is a zero-sum game. It is not the childhood game of cowboys and indians or even the occasional law-and-order action by our loyal policeman. In combat, it is winner-takes-all at the highest level. There is only one outcome when the two meet during that split-second blink of an eye and no choice of what level of force to be applied. It is the ultimate quick or the dead.

A combat soldier is truly an instrument of death. His sole purpose is to instantly take the life of another, which is the supreme objective. The rules of the jungle say that only one can live.

Combat is a contest of the senses: speed, accuracy, and effectiveness. The finality is who is left standing, who is taking the next breath. The combat soldier is programmed and wired to react, engage, and destroy with no thought, hesitancy, or misstep. The whole fabric of his being is to be a killing machine, an instrument of death. Born in training, molded in the fire of order, conditioned by action, and hardened by the rawness of survival. His very being is bound to the one universal drive of all creatures, that of the survival of the fittest. Fighting to kill—to kill the enemy before he kills you. It is to kill in order to live. To be faster, smarter, quicker, stronger, and better equipped. It is the dance of death.

SOLDIER'S FRIEND

My brother
could have died
in 'Nam, but
he cleaned his
rifle on schedule,
chopped his own
path through the jungle,
and watched for "Charlie"
even in his sleep.
He also talked a lot
to a friend called
God.

—Allen Field Weitzel
May 14, 1980
1:18 A.M.
For Warren

25-METER TARGET

The target
looked
like a man
scattered
over vermilion sky.
Having direction
before death;
expressing color
going down.
The paper spoke
too loud
of a man
once behind a rifle;
gone now.
Alone
in the fact
that man
is a target
always.

—Allen Field Weitzel
April 15, 1968
10:37 P.M.
For David E. Kline

VIETNAM LETTERS, 1966–1980

Always answered your
Mekong Delta letters
with poems from home.
Length of your letters
controlled by the size
of your "C" ration box
stationery. You always
remarked about the clear
star-stuffed skies, without city lights to
blur one's vision of heaven (a place you
always prayed to, while
.223-millimeter slugs
slammed into dirt, inches
from your muddy, shaking knees.)
Years older and poems wiser,
you returned safely home,
because we all prayed to God
or because some V.C.
was a lousy shot.

—Allen Field Weitzel
December 15, 1979
2:24 A.M.
For Warren and Dave

ABOUT THE AUTHOR

Warren P. Weitzel, 2009. (Photo: Author's collection)

Warren has spent fifty years of FUN! FUN! FUN! in the amusement and recreation field, with the last 29 years as the director of operations at the Winchester Mystery House in San Jose, California. Warren was already working in the industry while attending San Jose State University. It was during this time period that he was drafted.

As a widower, Warren's home is lively as he spends time watching the antics of his two raccoons, Happy and Jingles. They live nearby in the Almaden Quicksilver Park and they stop by daily to eat and visit.

Warren is an avid investor involved in three successful investment clubs. He spends his leisure time reading the classics from his vast library.

The younger of the two Weitzel brothers, Allen, is a writer and has worked in the same industry for forty-five years.

Warren's son, Tim, and his wife Jennifer, live in Texas along with Warren's granddaughter, Samantha.

You may contact Warren or Allen through the Weitzel website: www. witent.com.